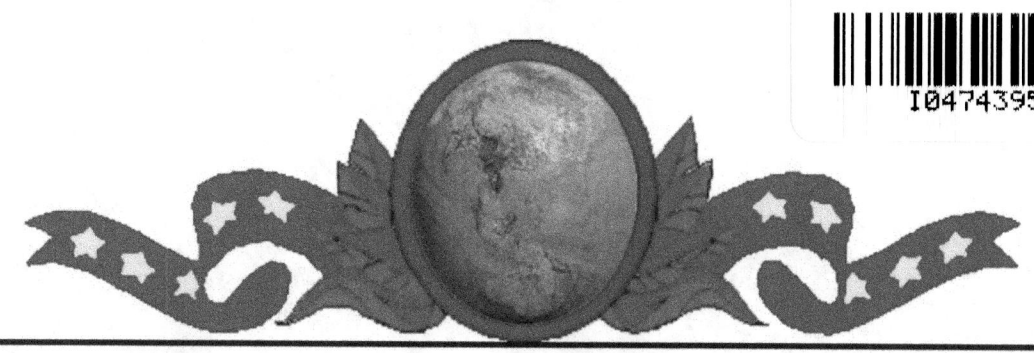

Real World Colouring Book
For Advanced Users & Adults

Copyright 2019 By John Boom

50 Images

**Created From Real Life Photos
For You To Colour As You Please.**

ISBN 978-0-359-78817-0

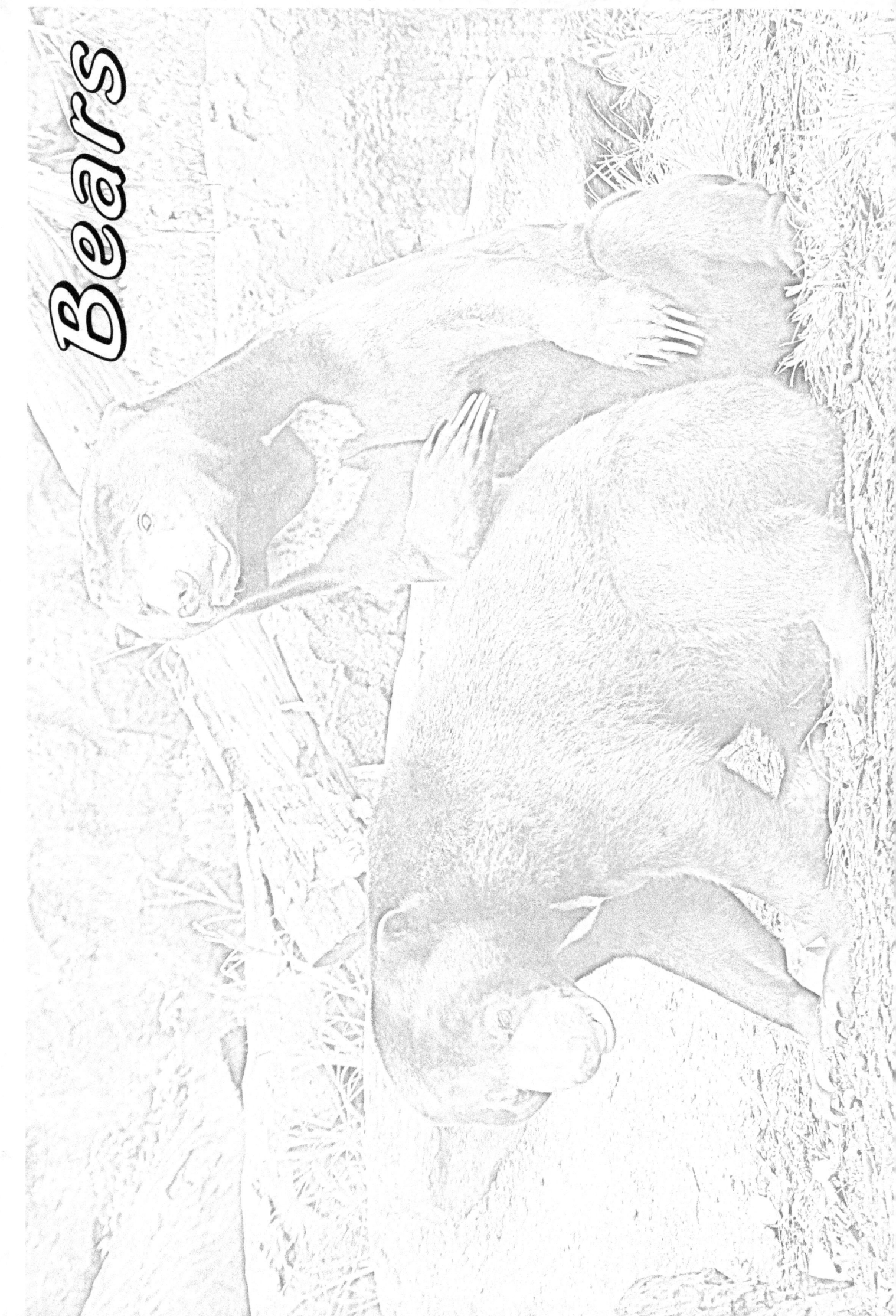

Bears

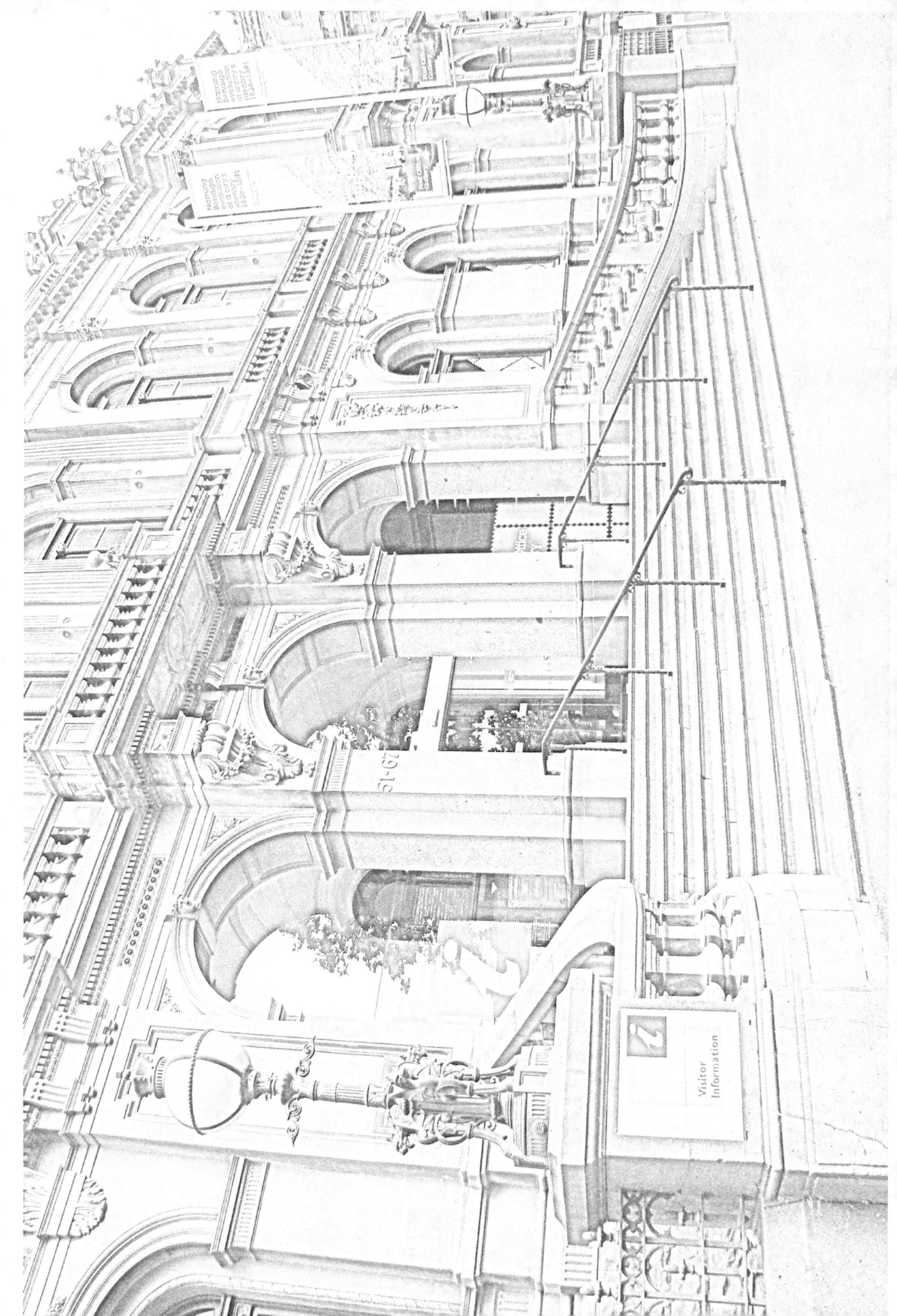

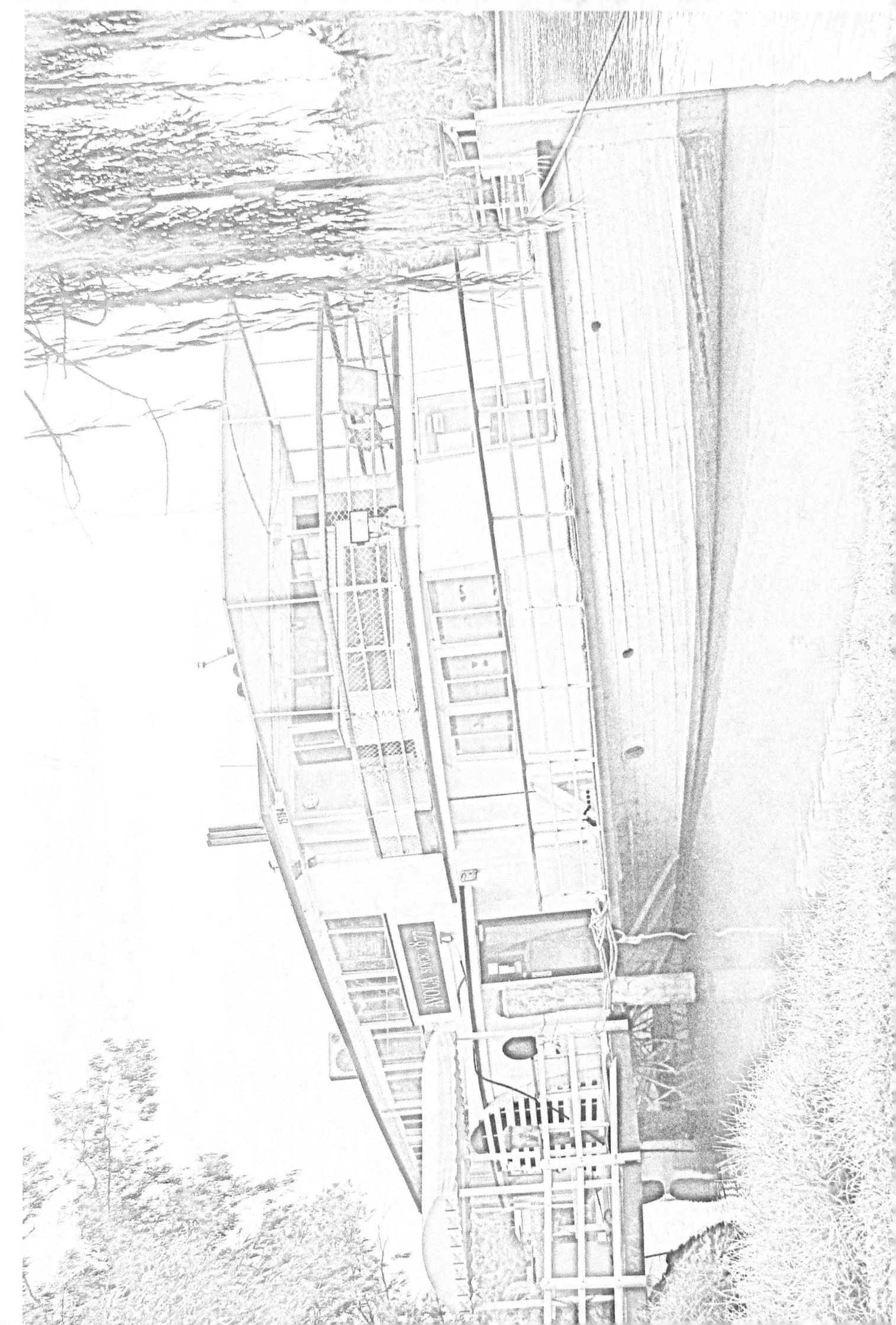

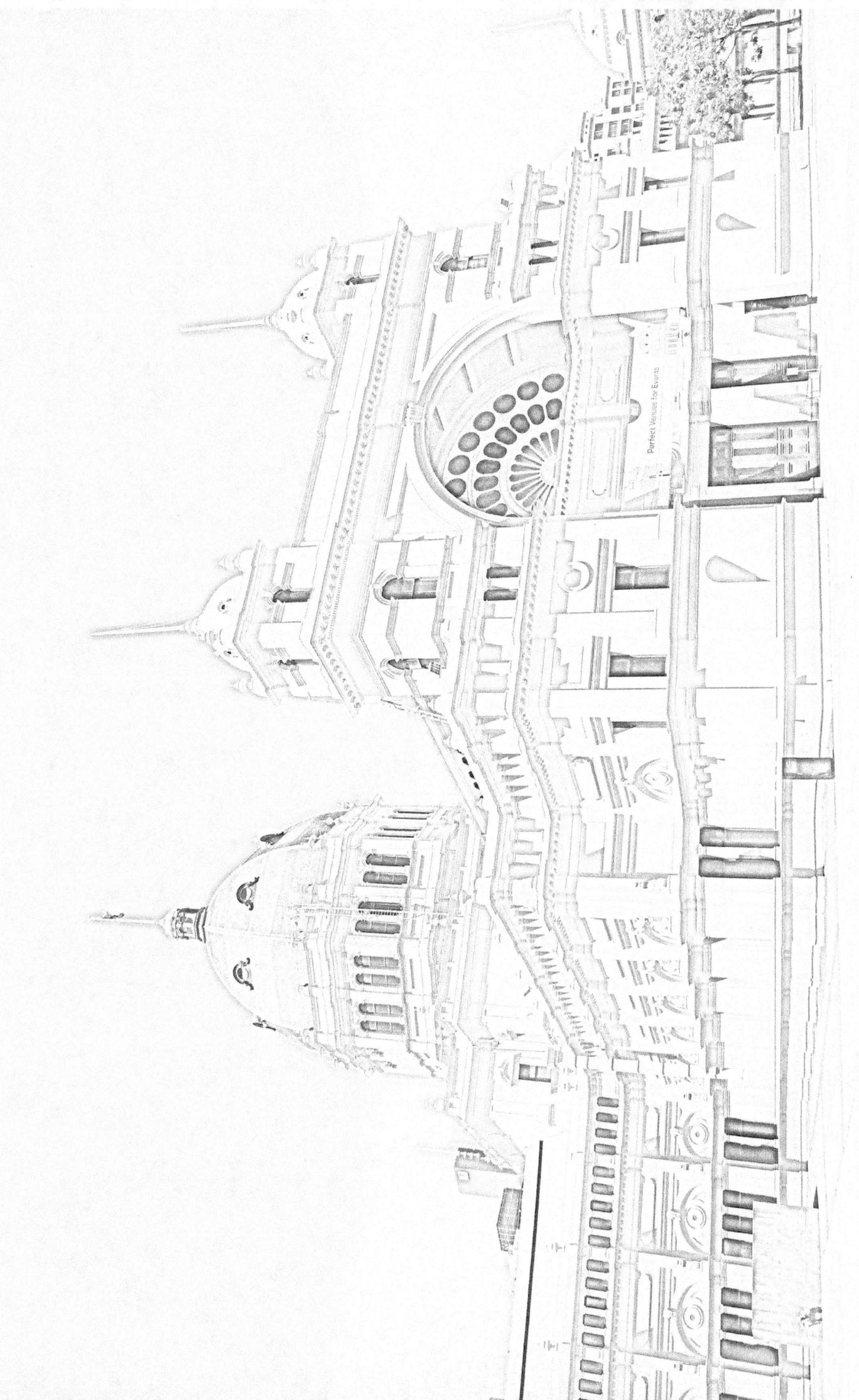

Perfect Venues for Events

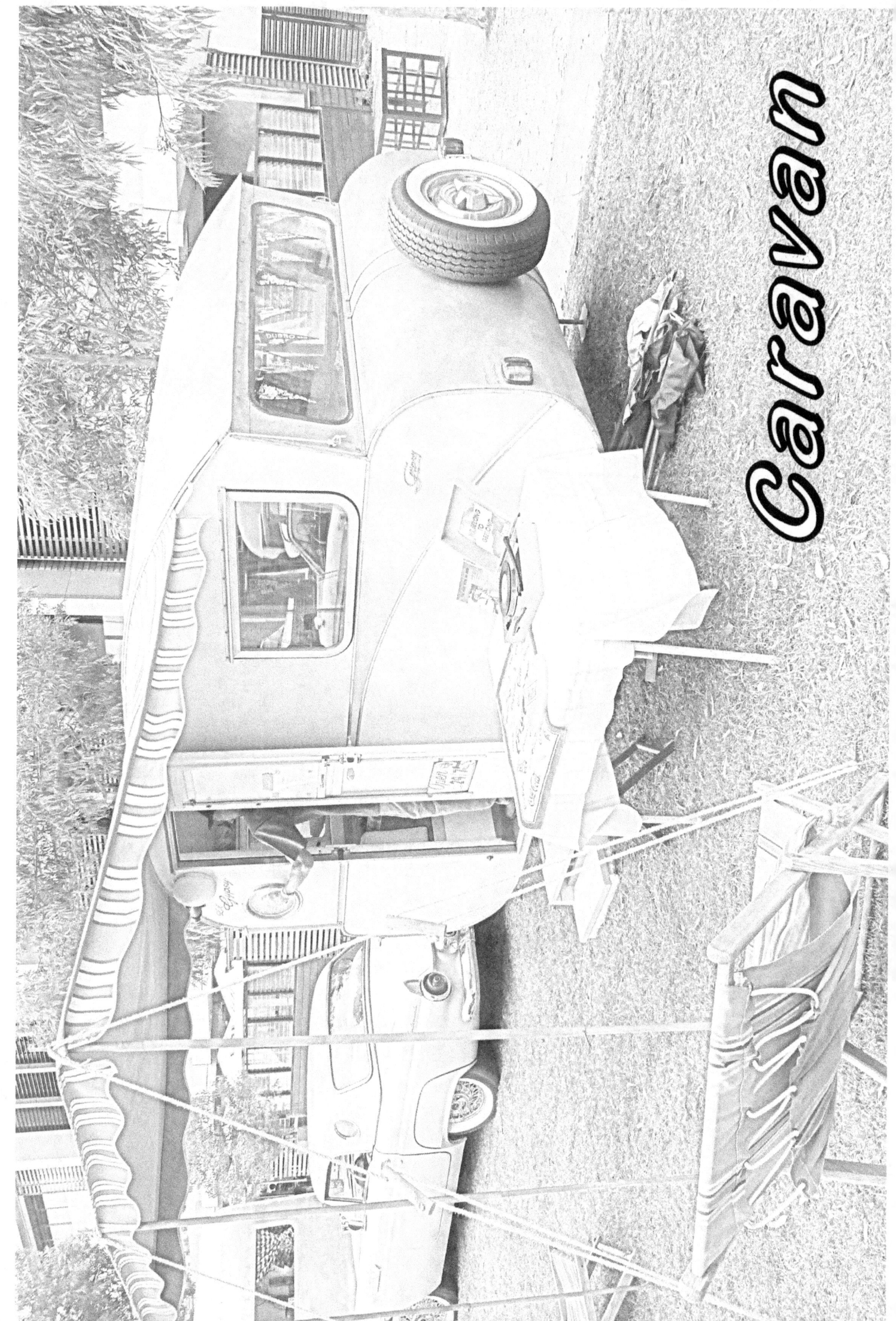

Caravan

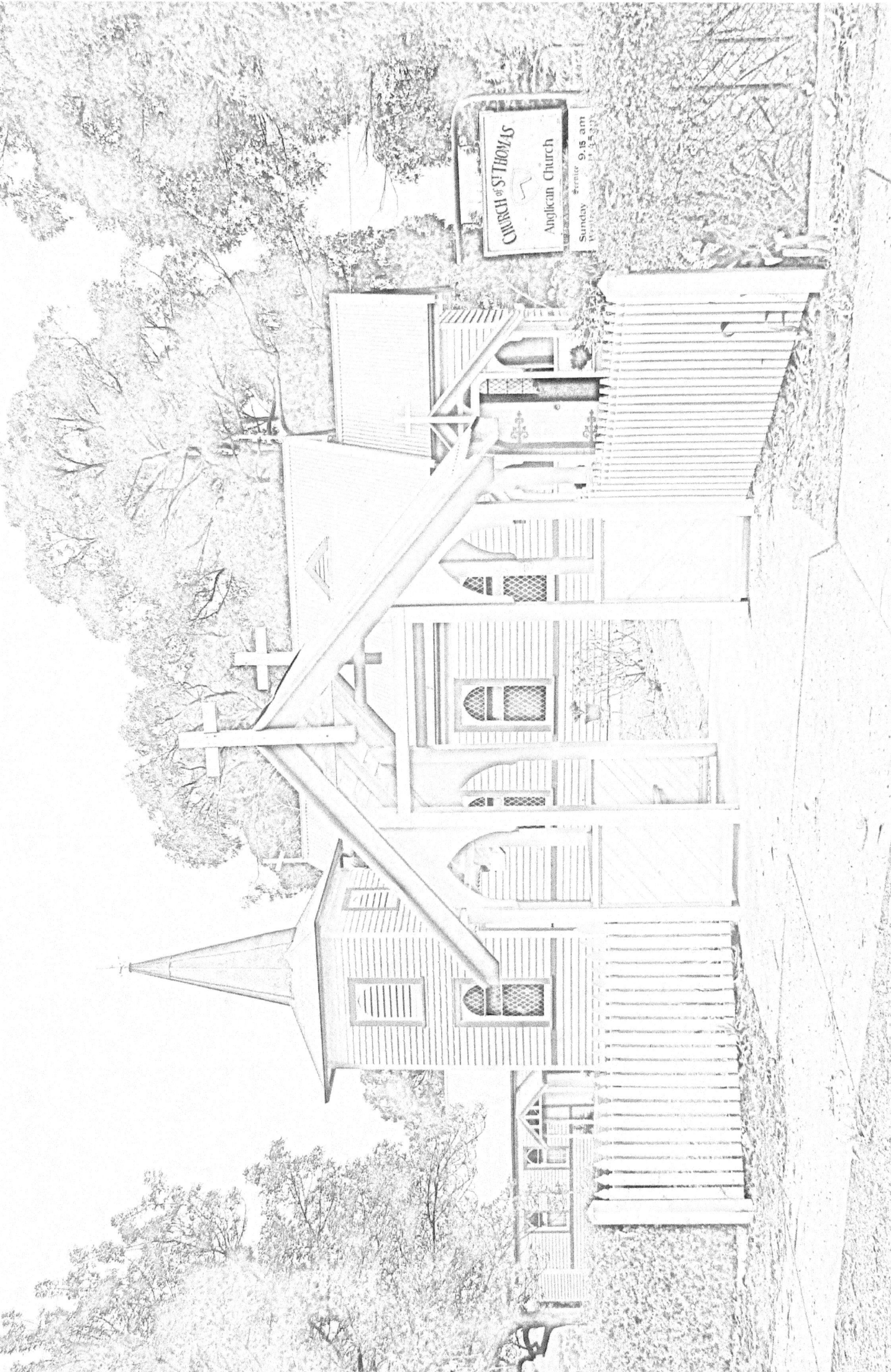

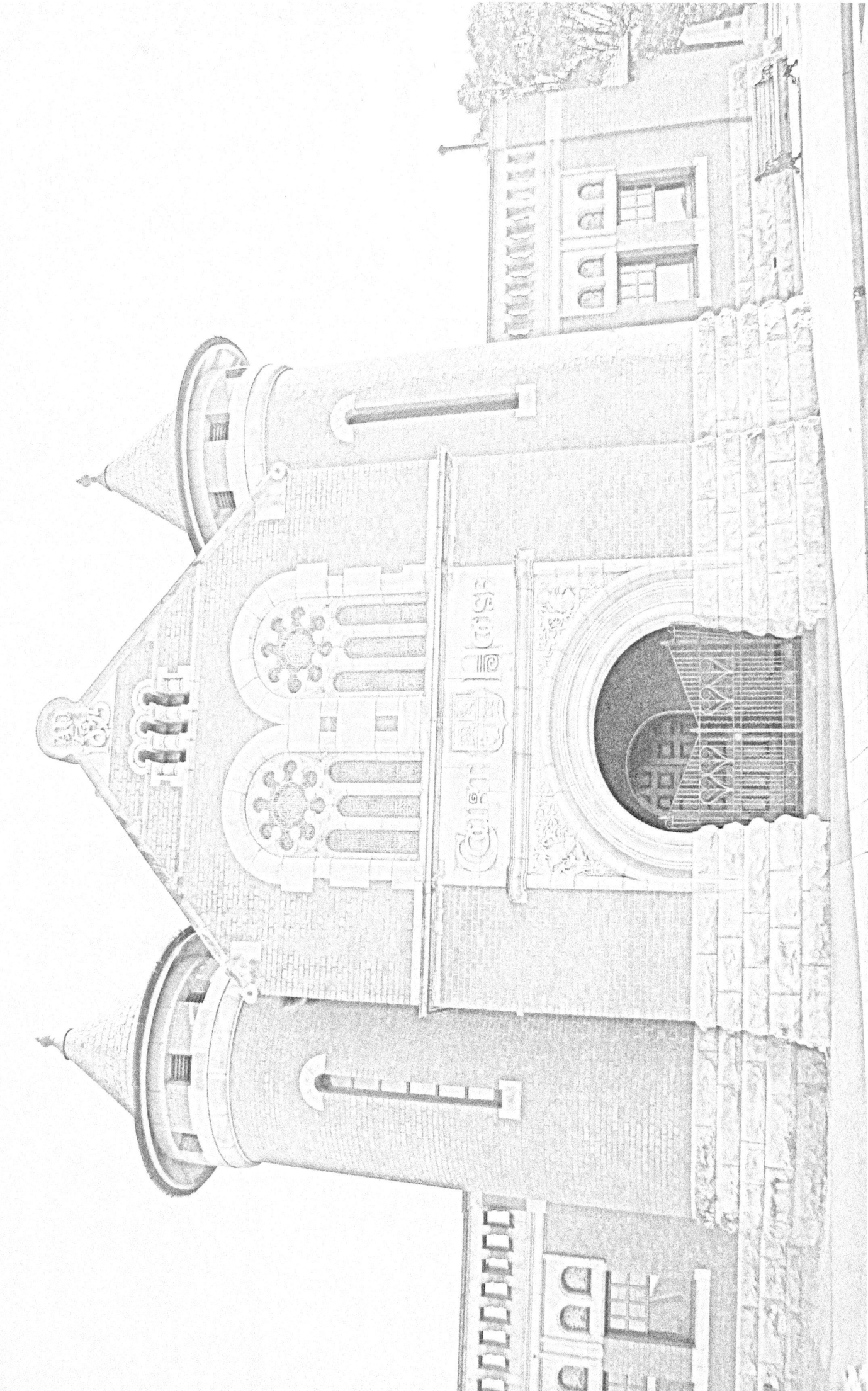

Crocodile

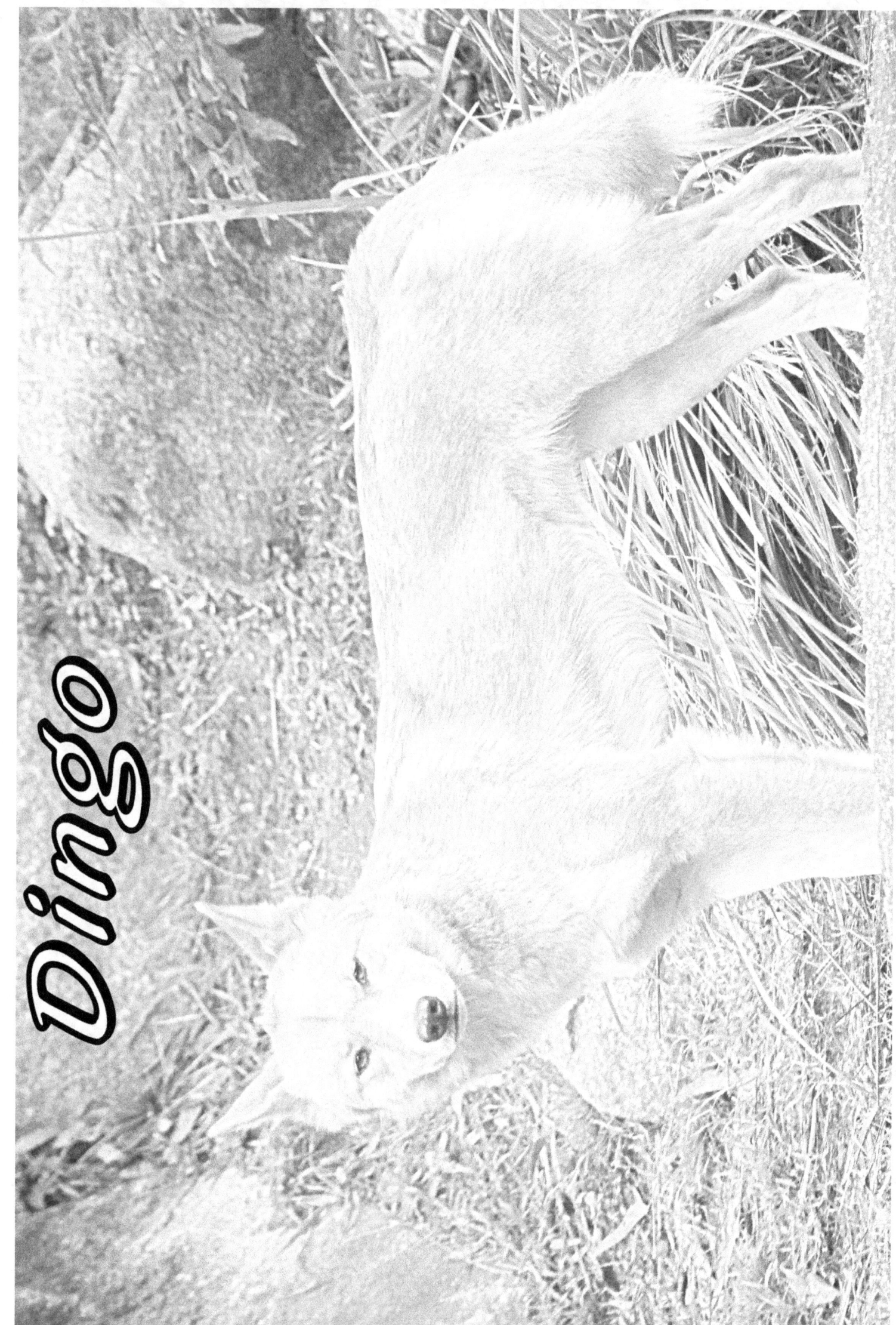

Dingo

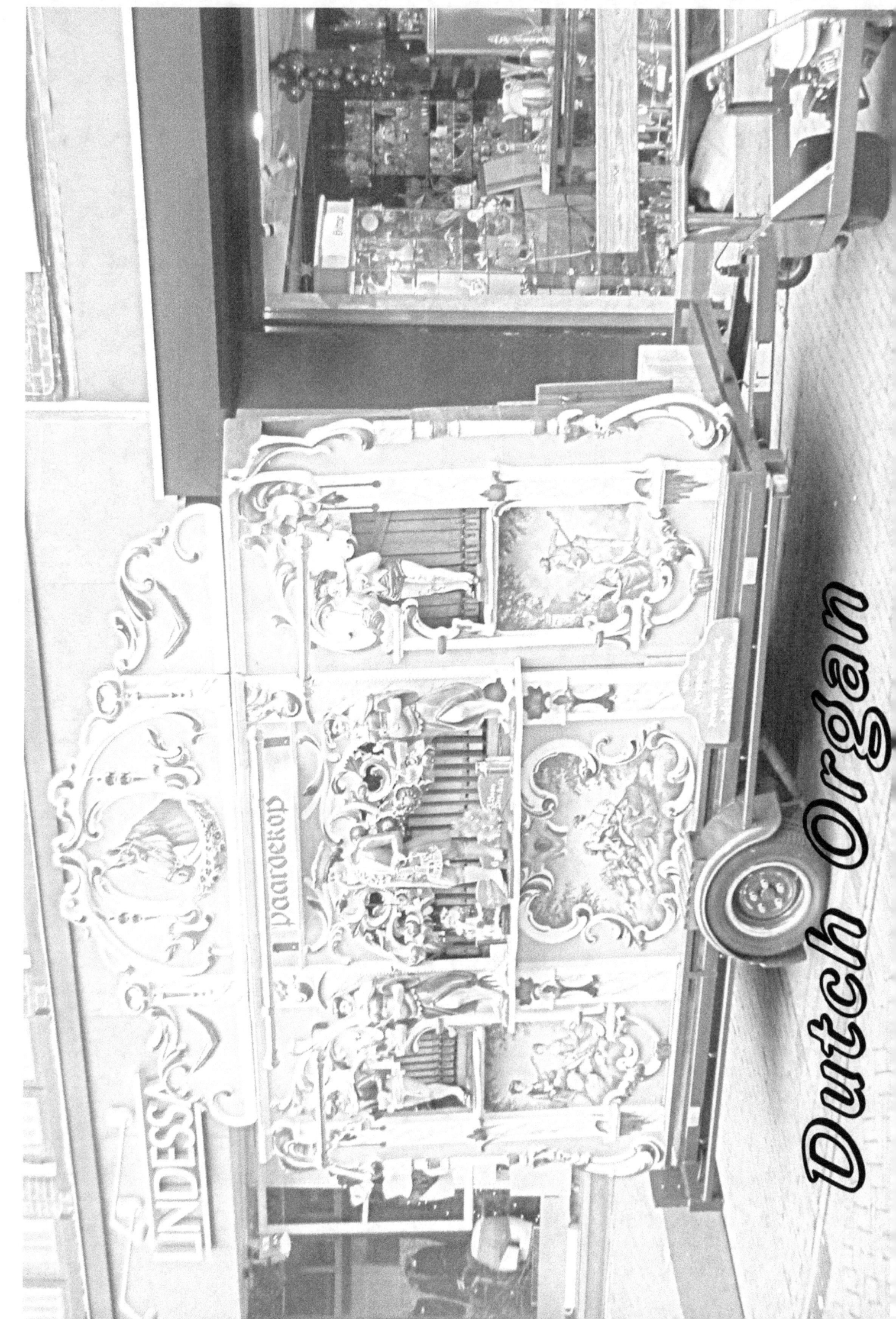

Dutch Organ

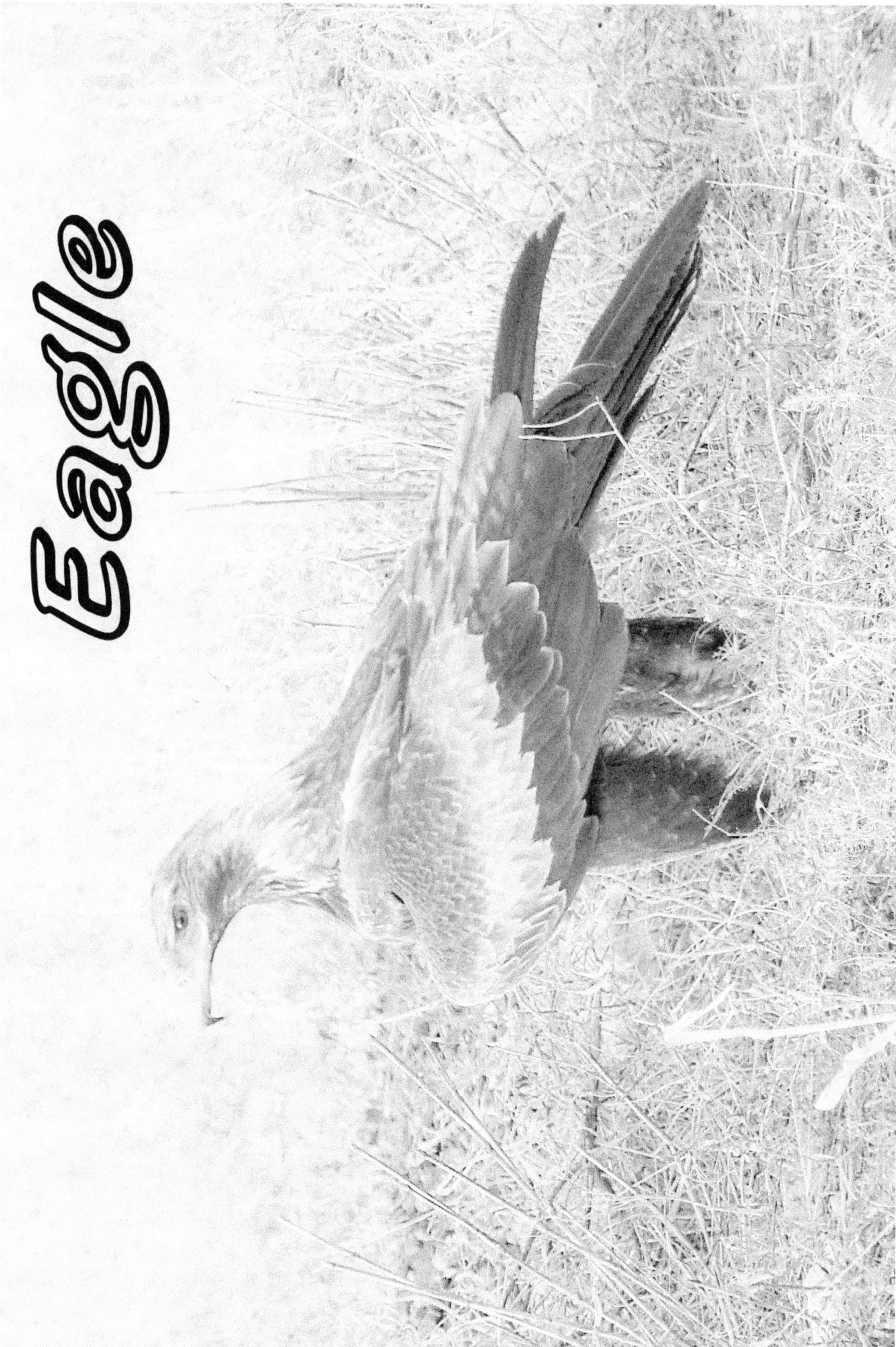

Eagle

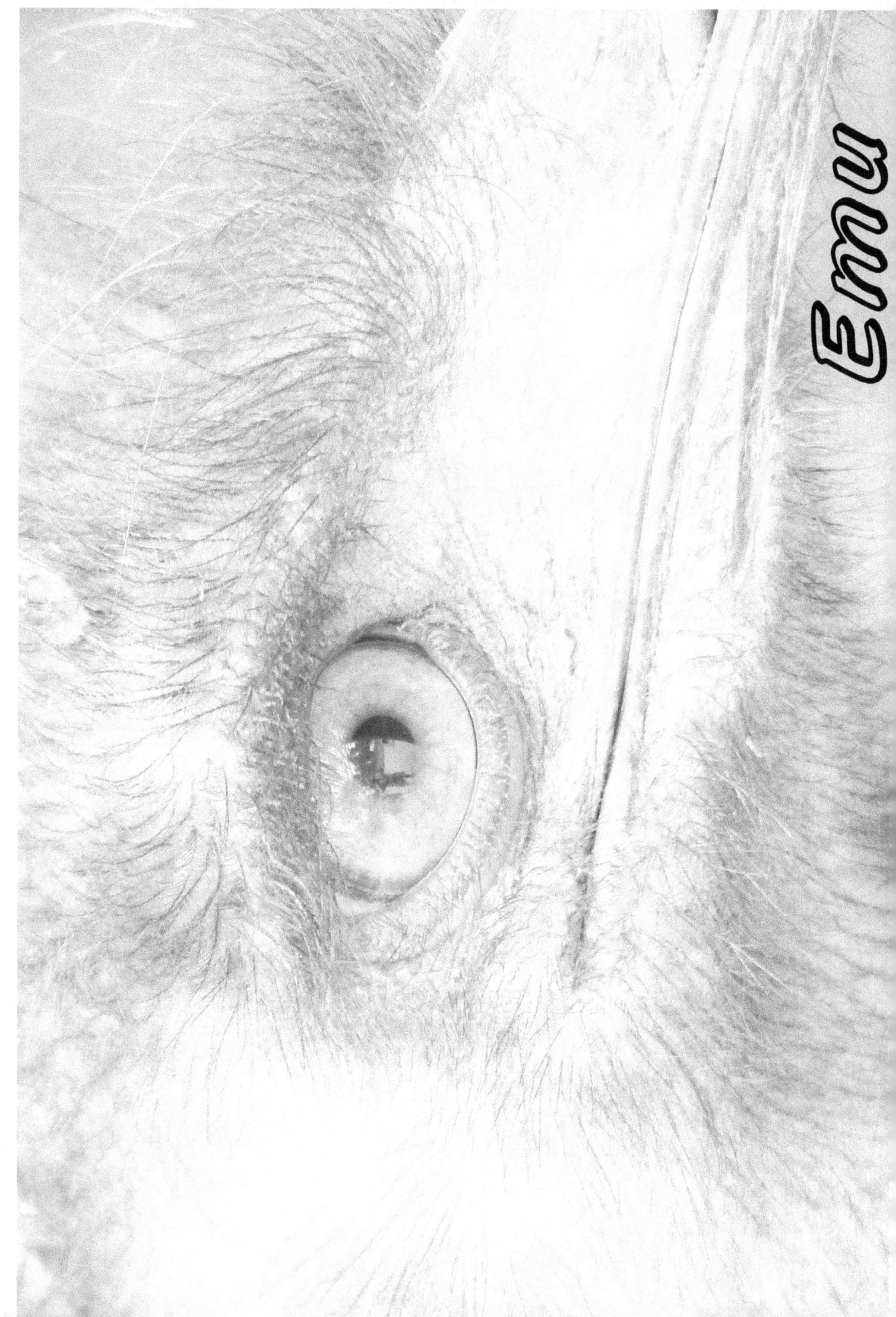

Emu

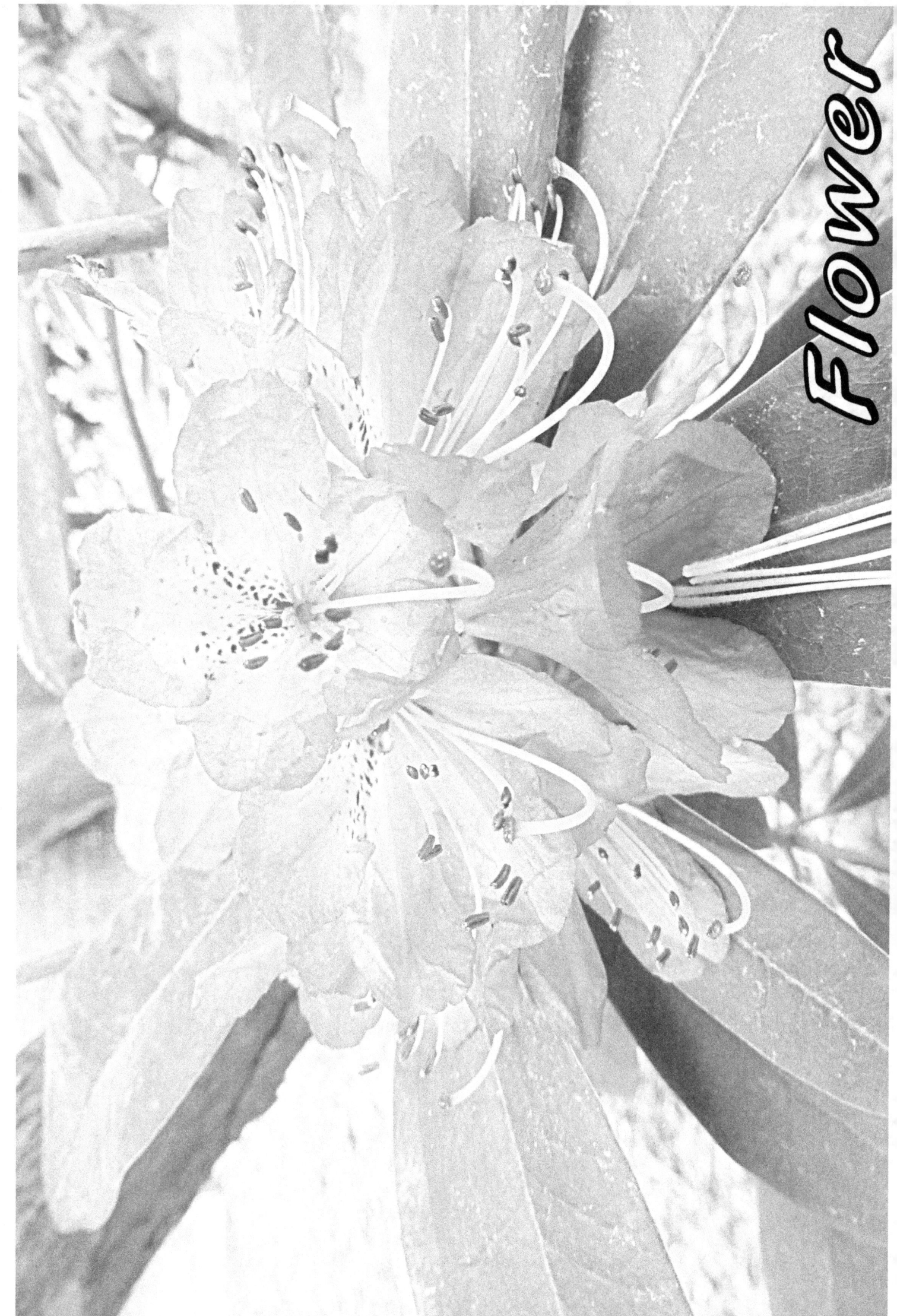
Flower

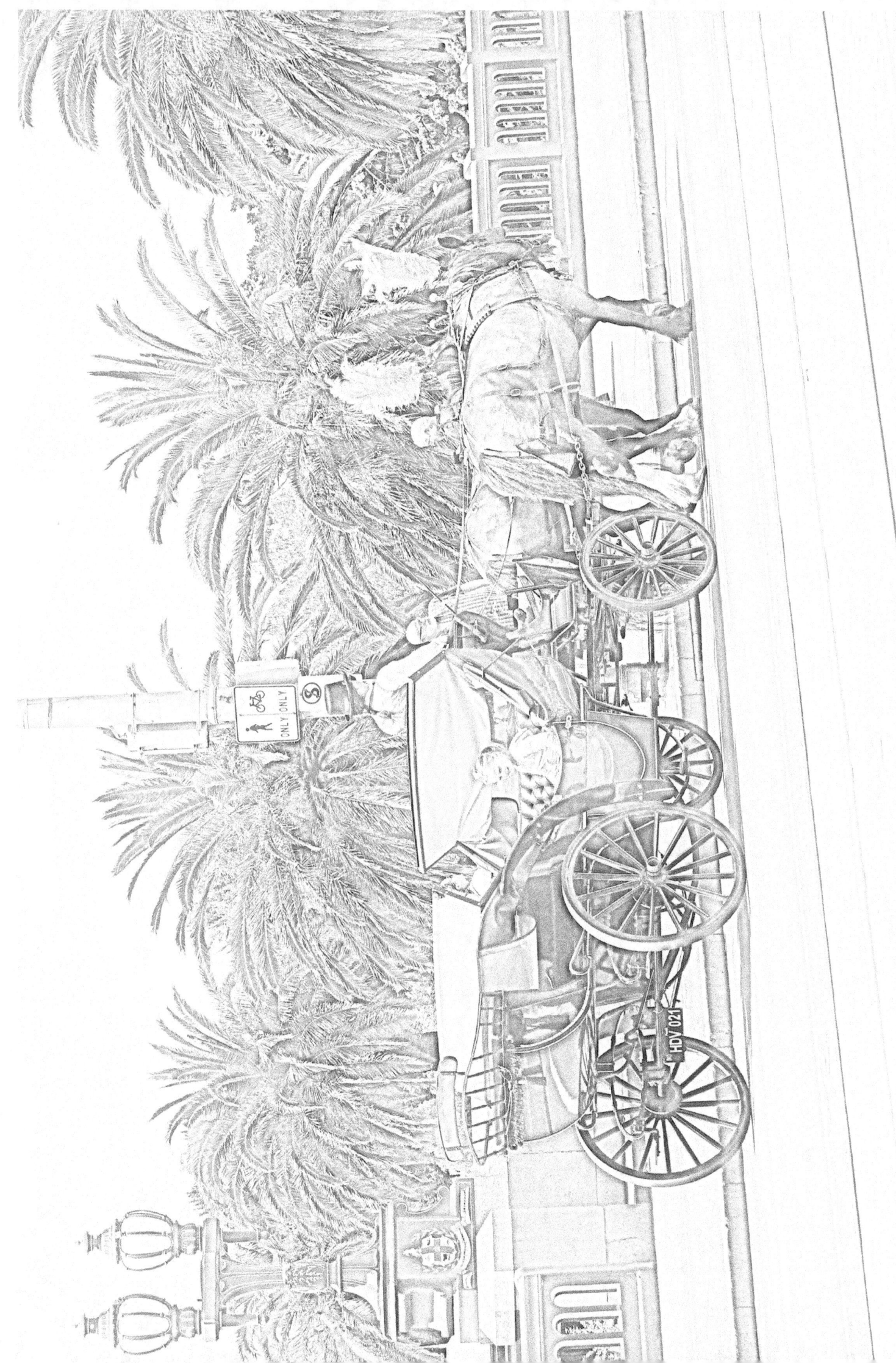

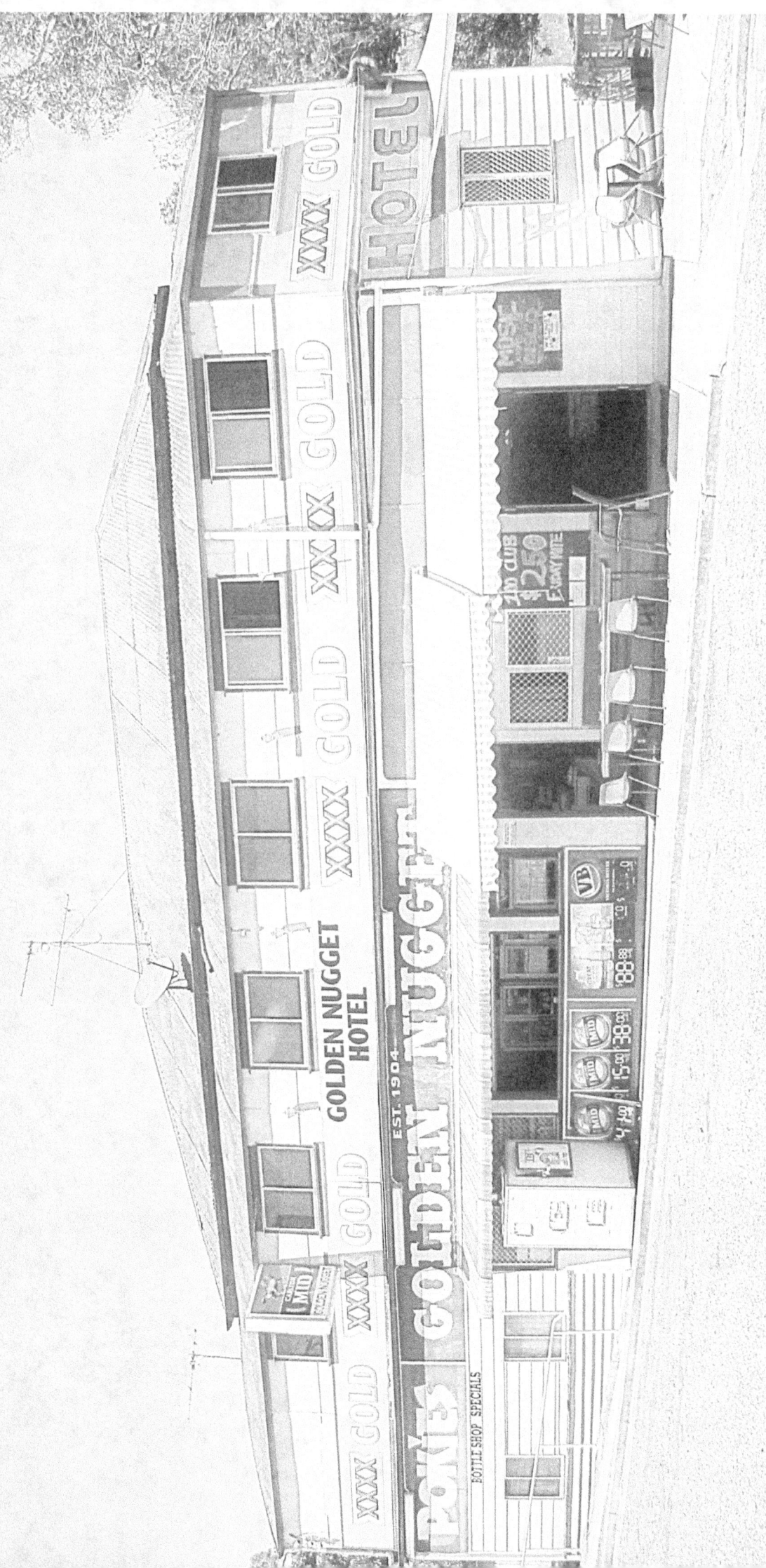

Hotel

Hotel

Hotel

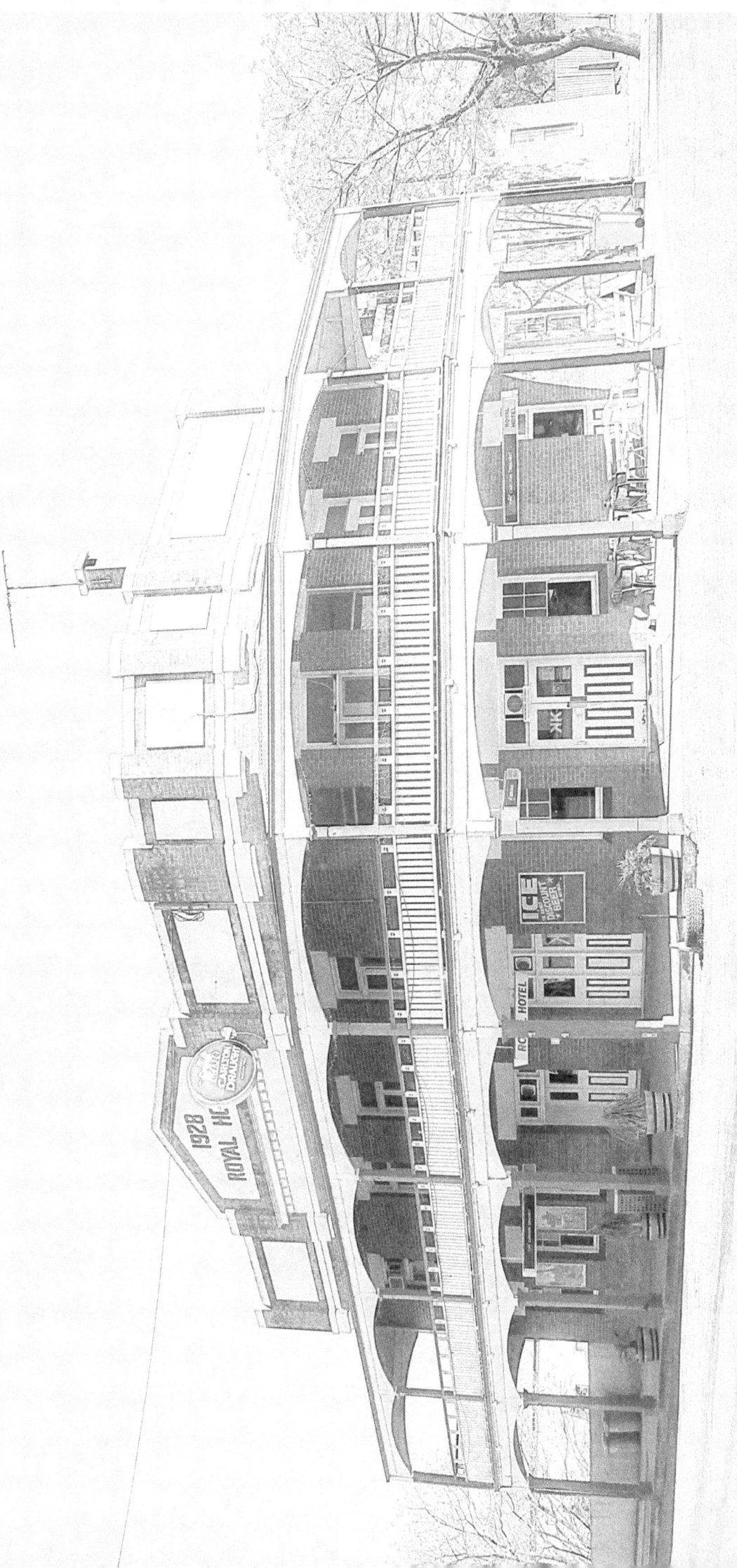

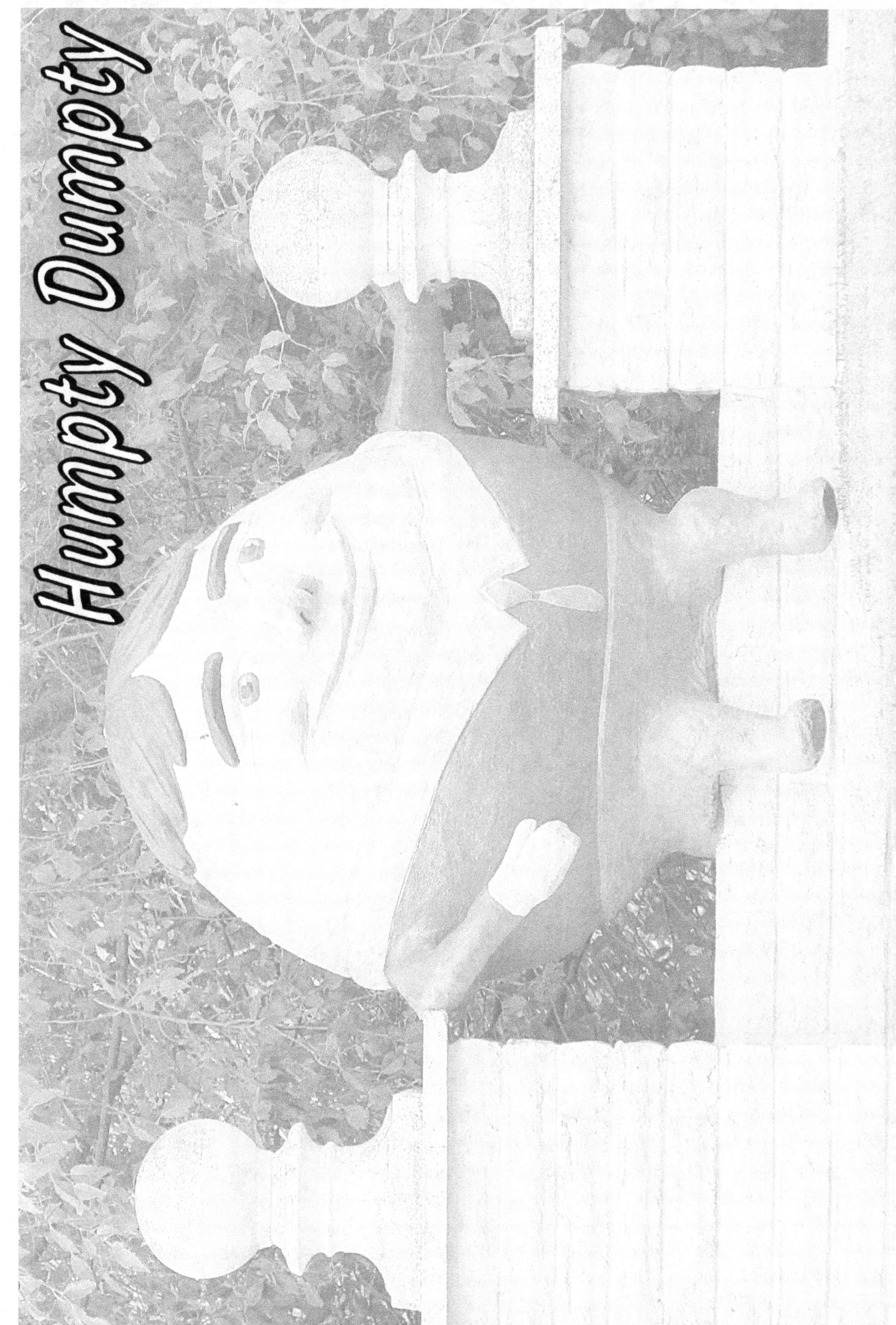

Humpty Dumpty

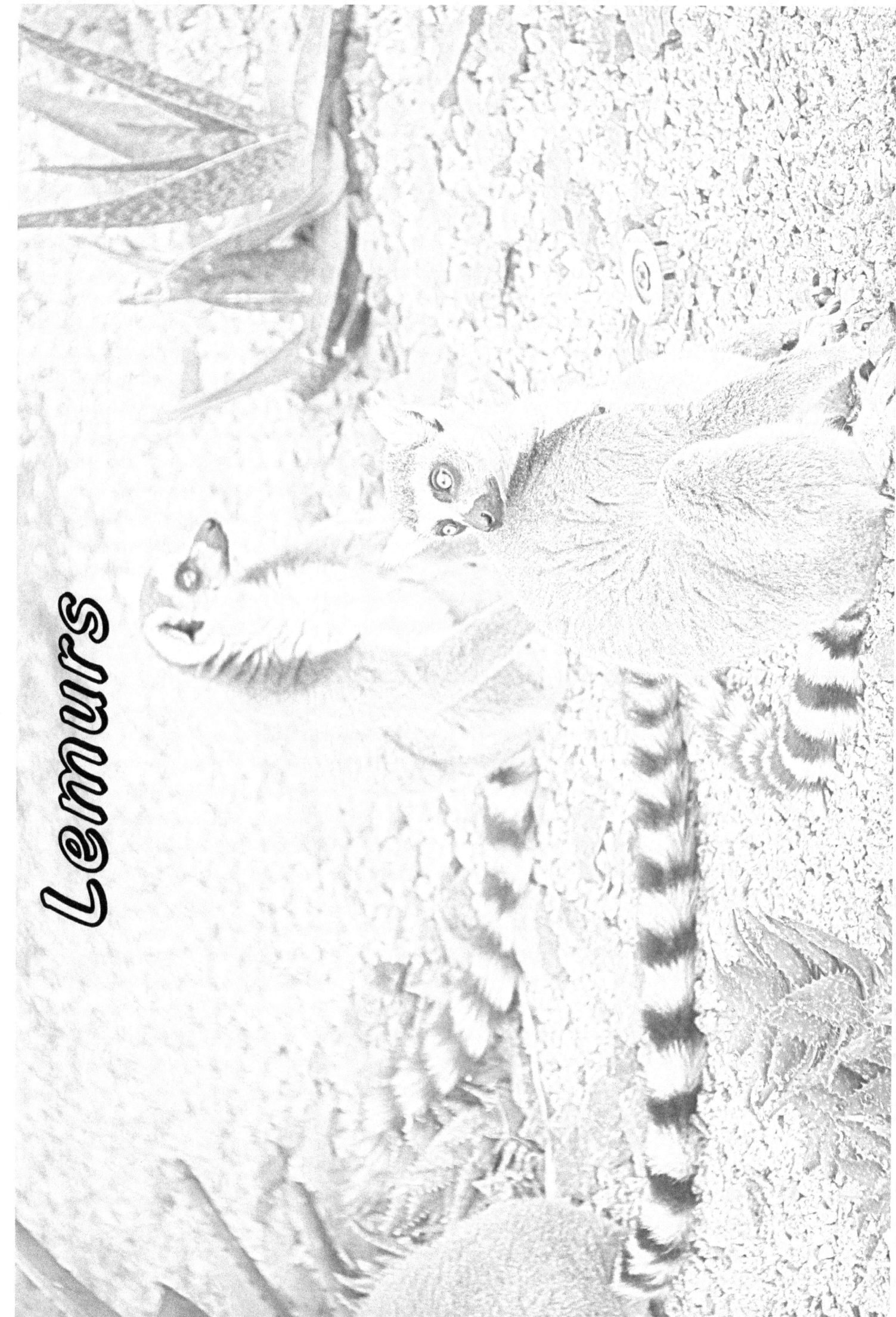

Lemurs

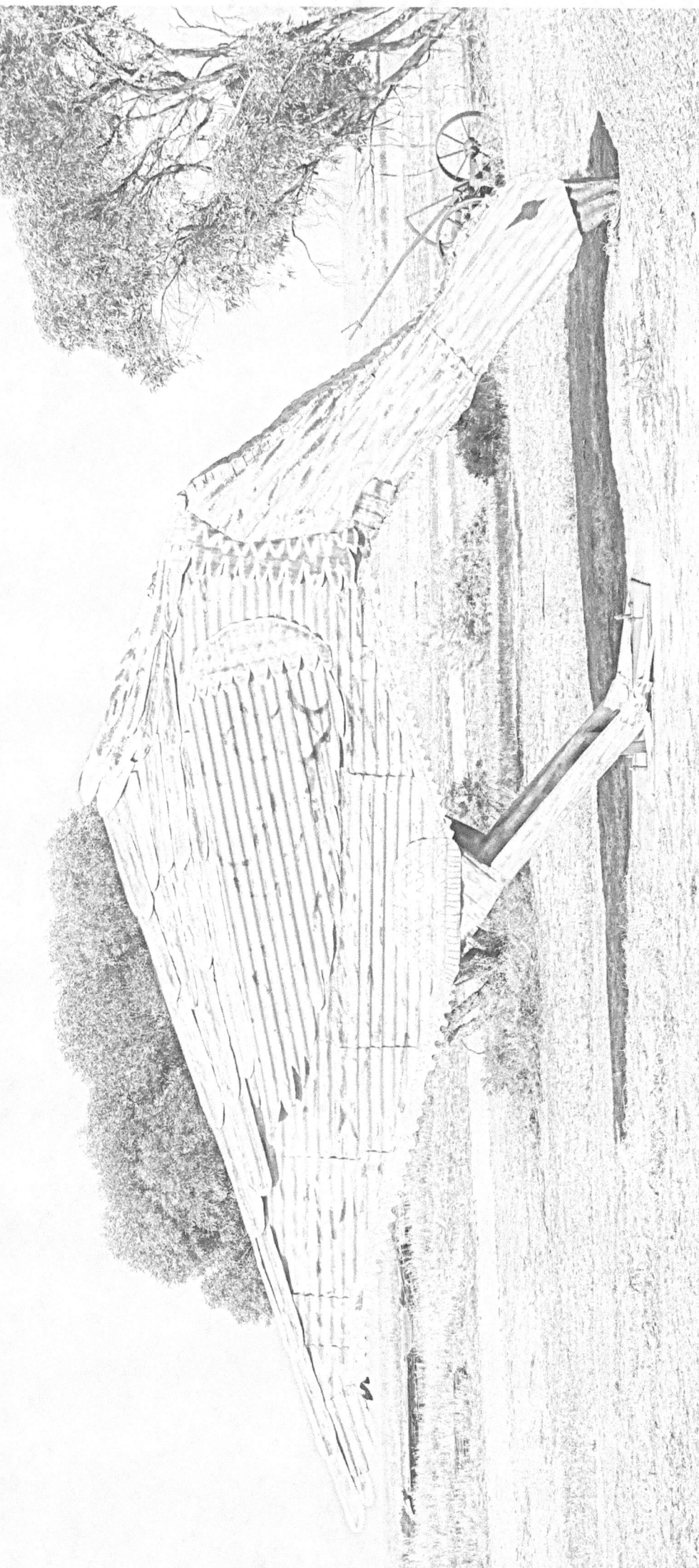

Big Mallee Fowl

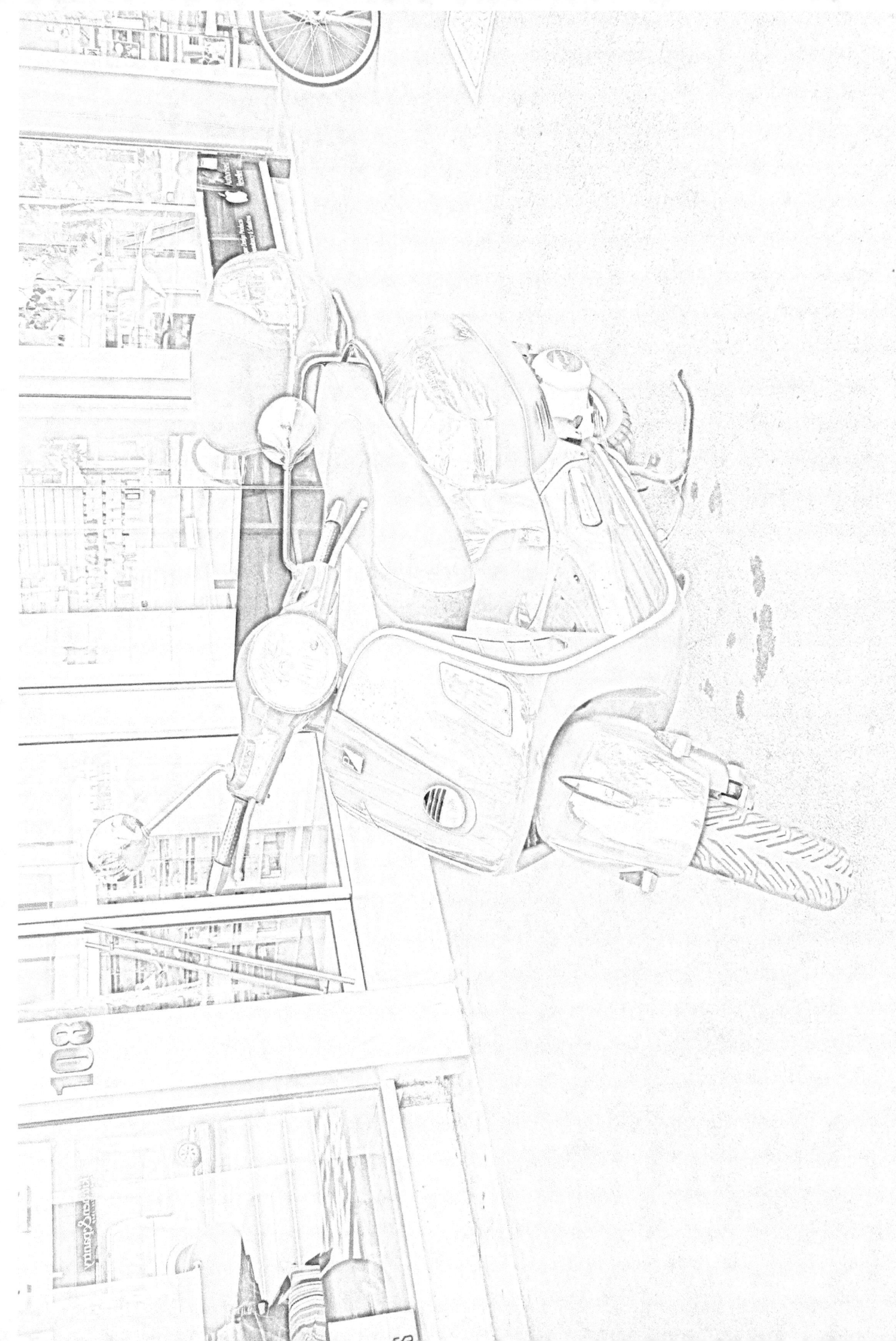

Museum

Orangutan

Panda Bear

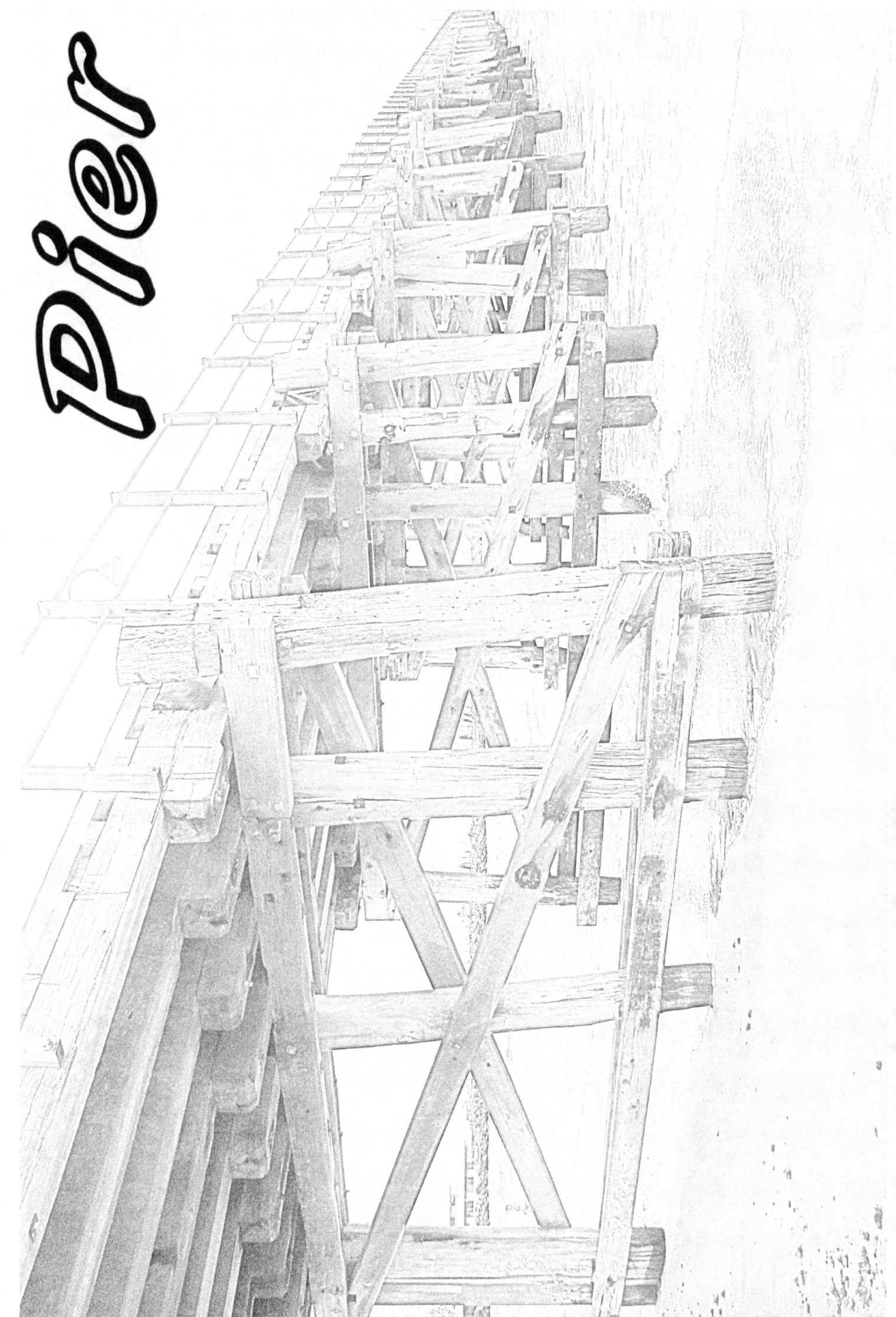

Pier

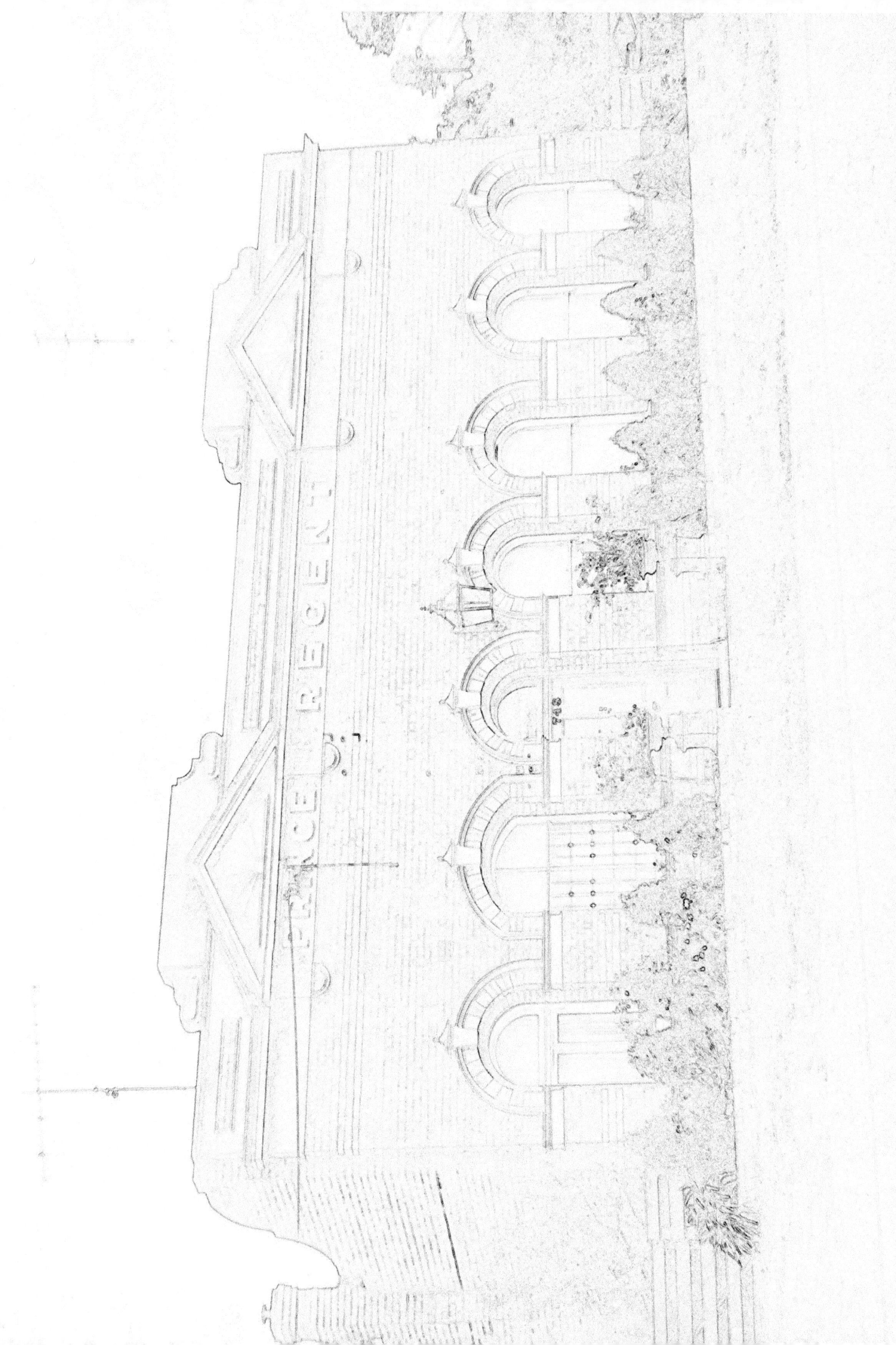

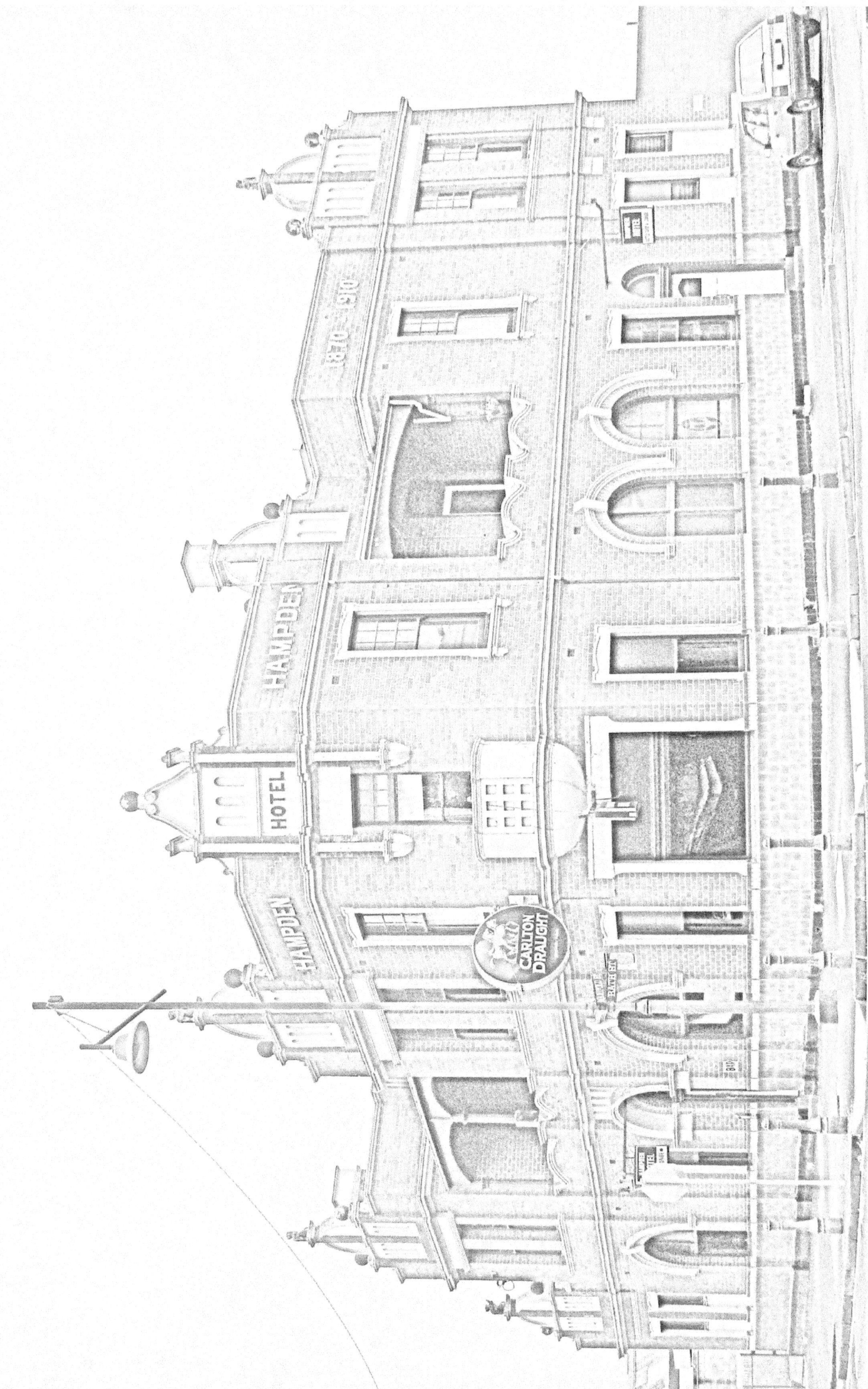

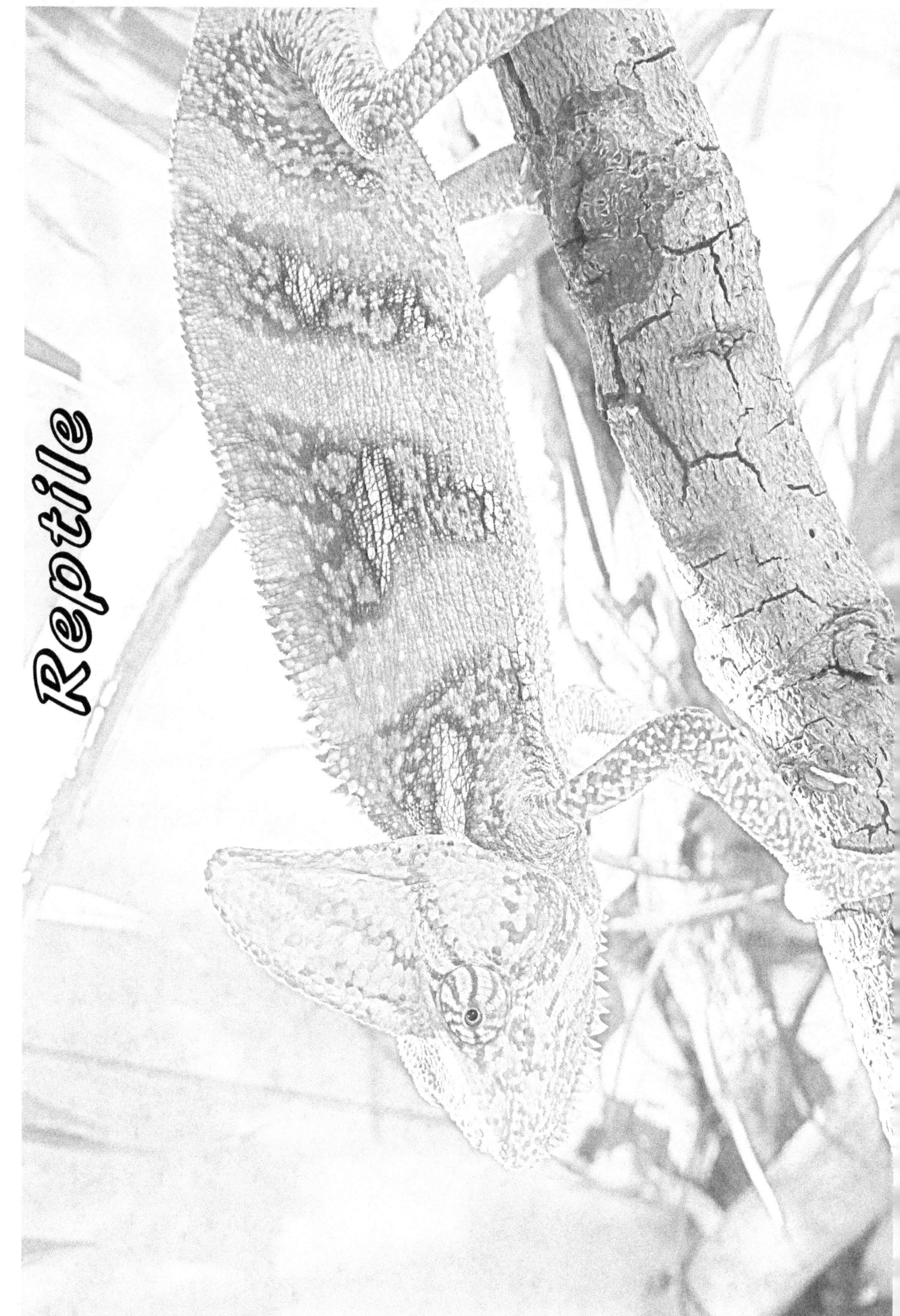

Reptile

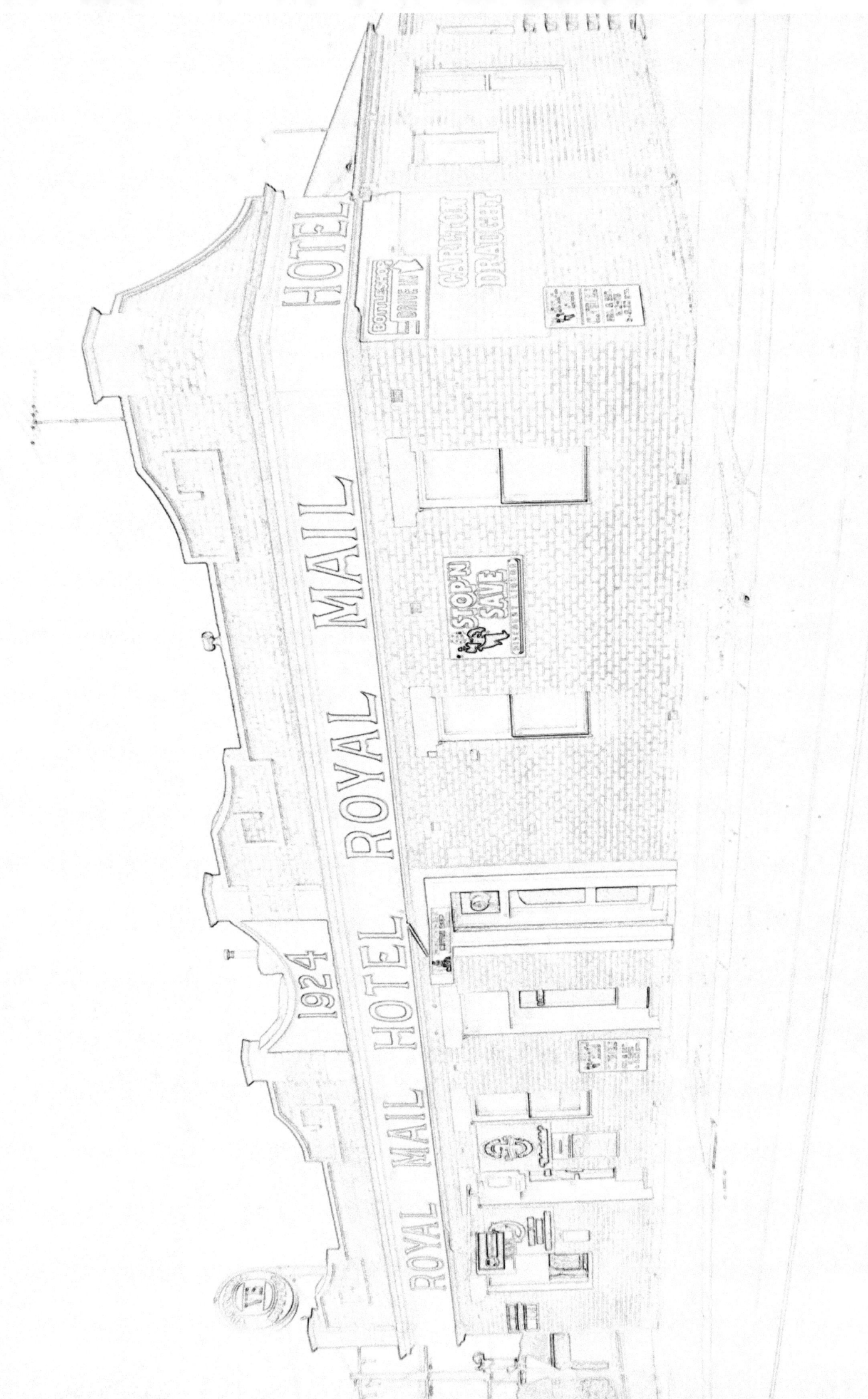

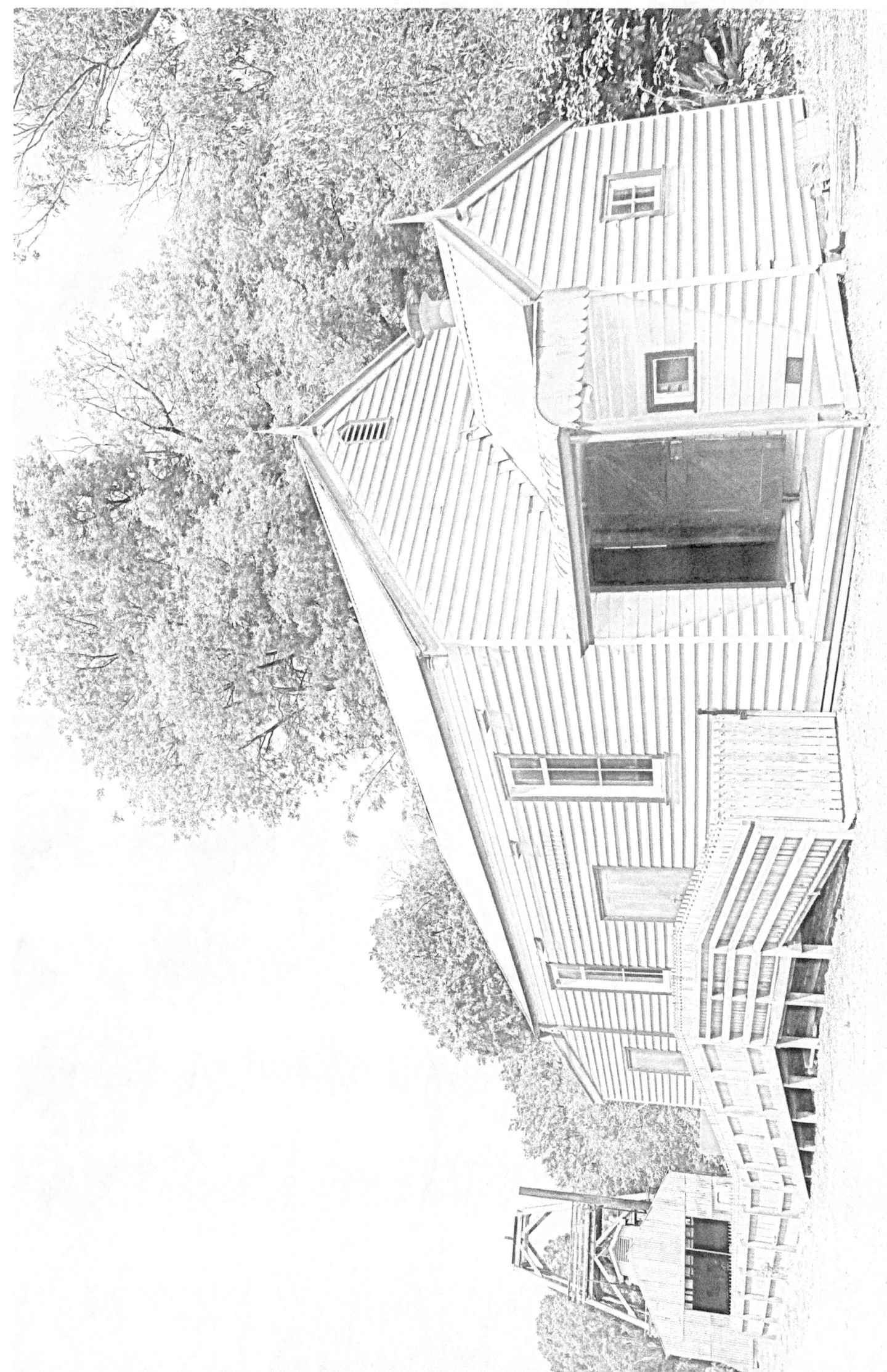

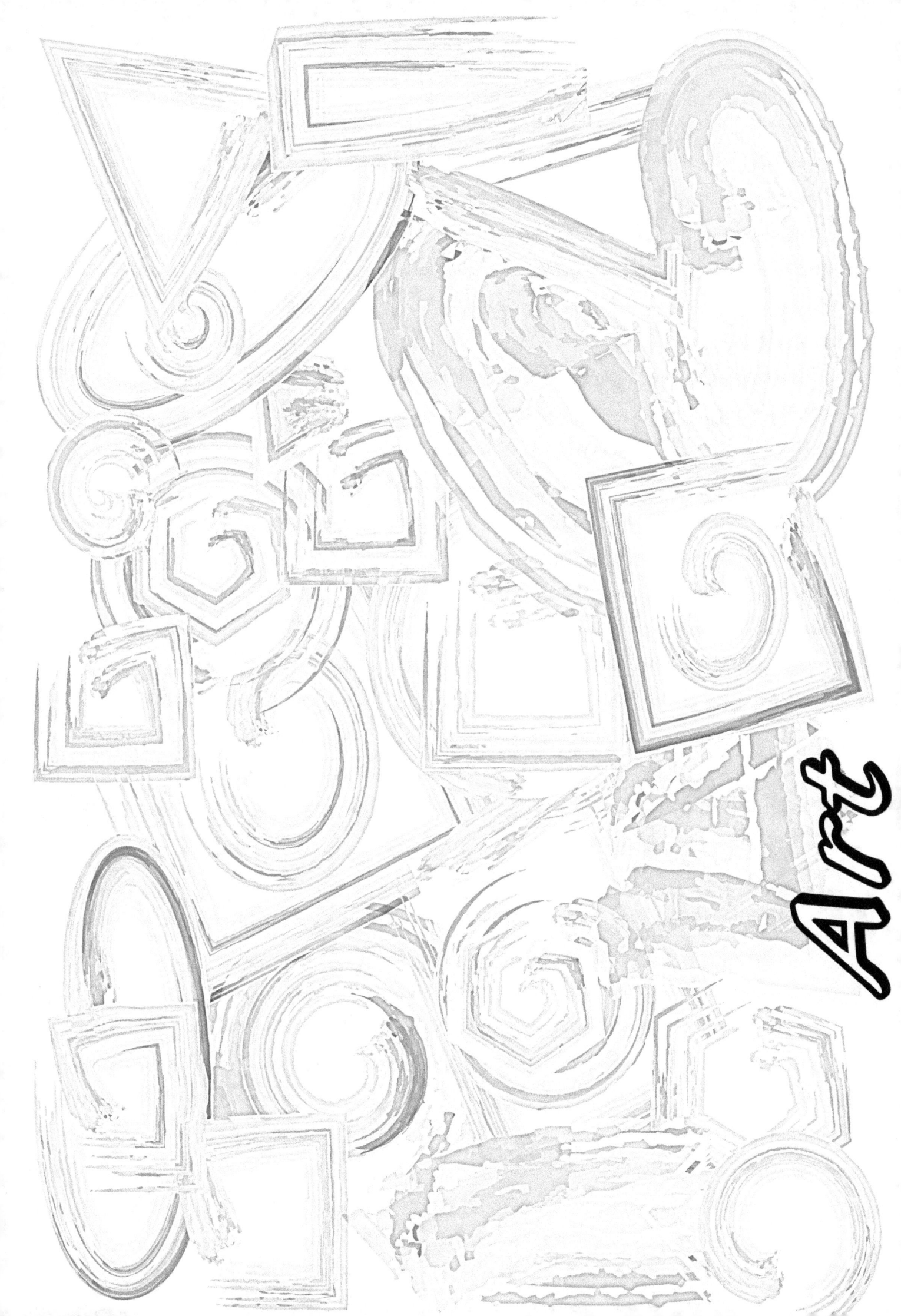

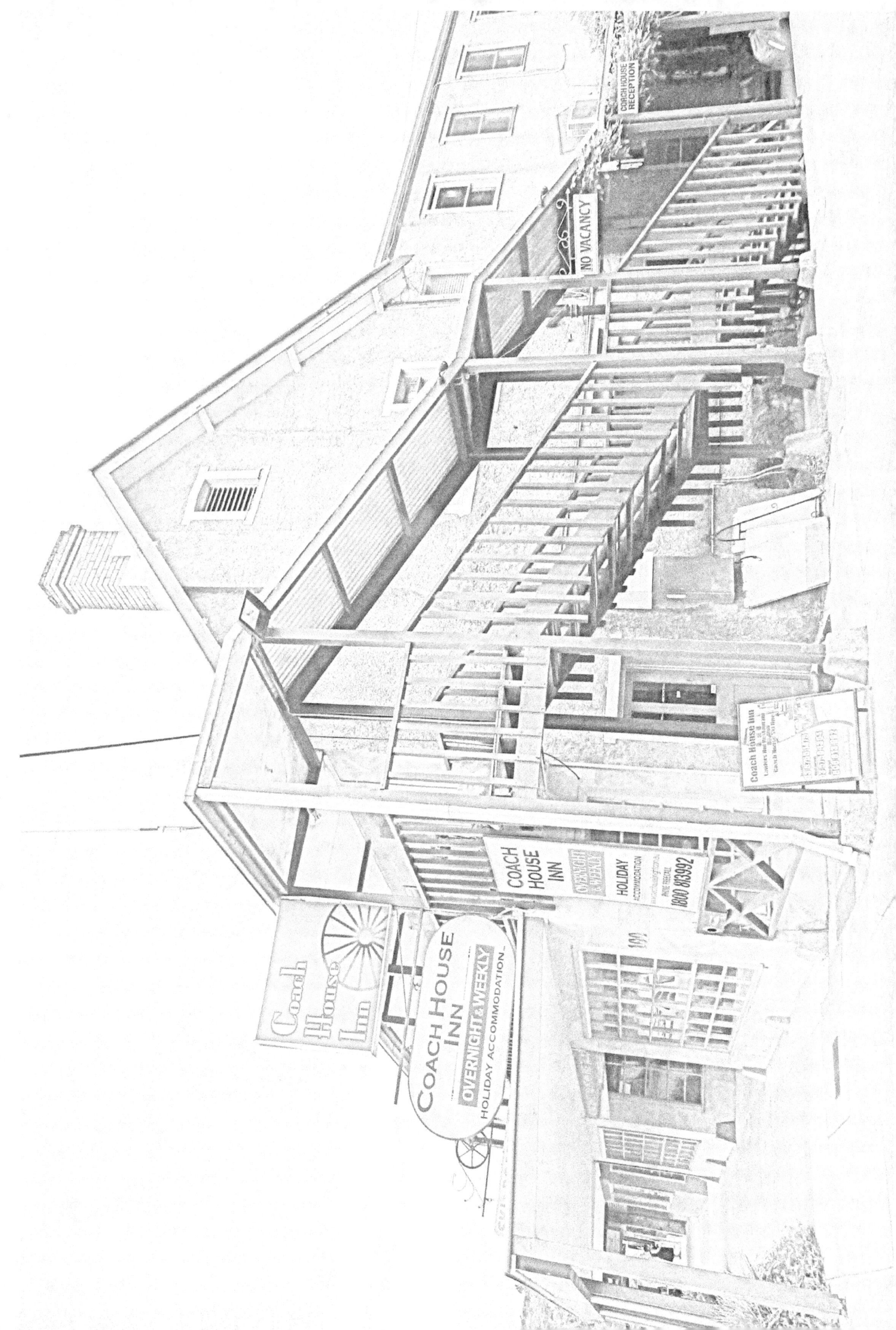

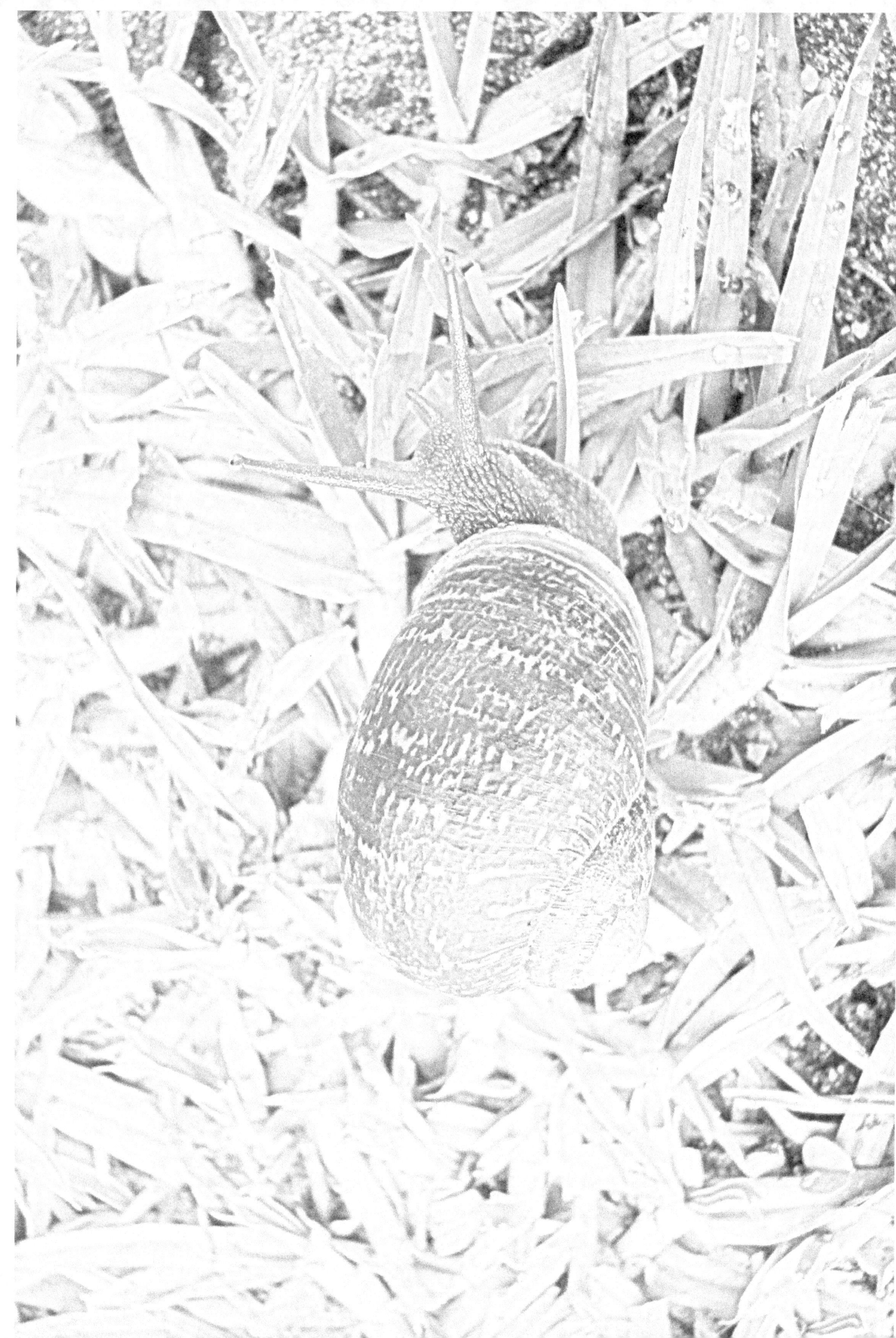

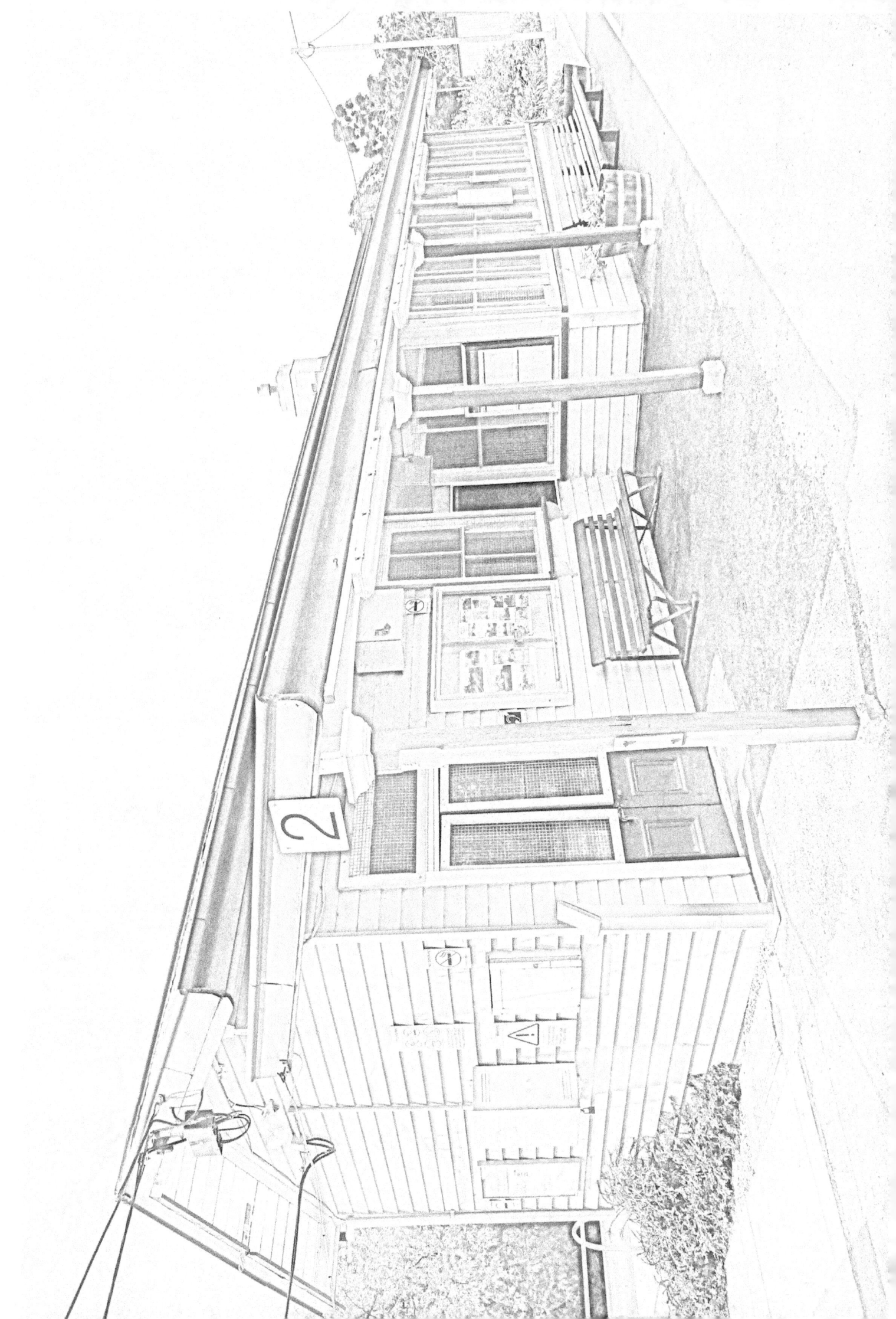

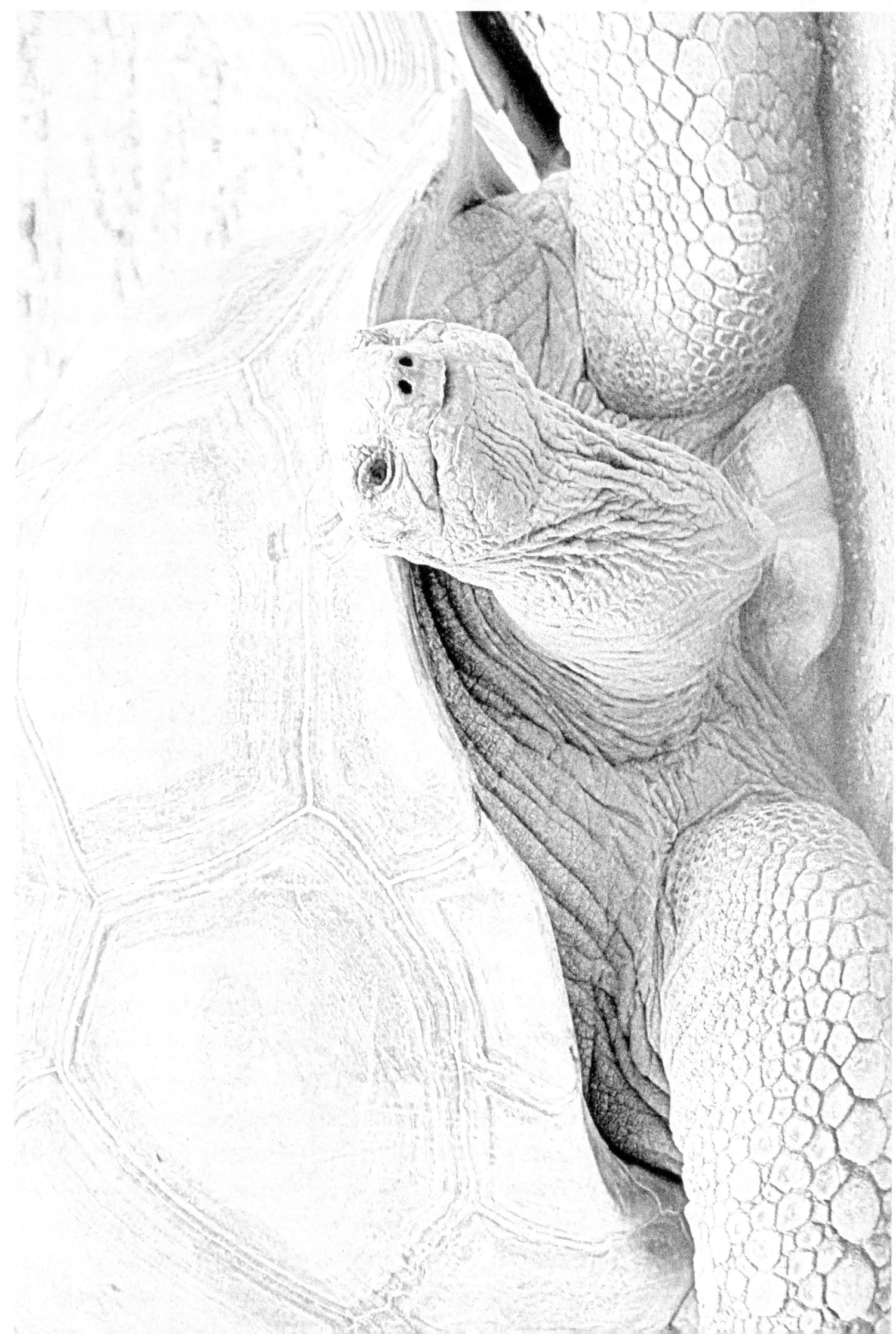

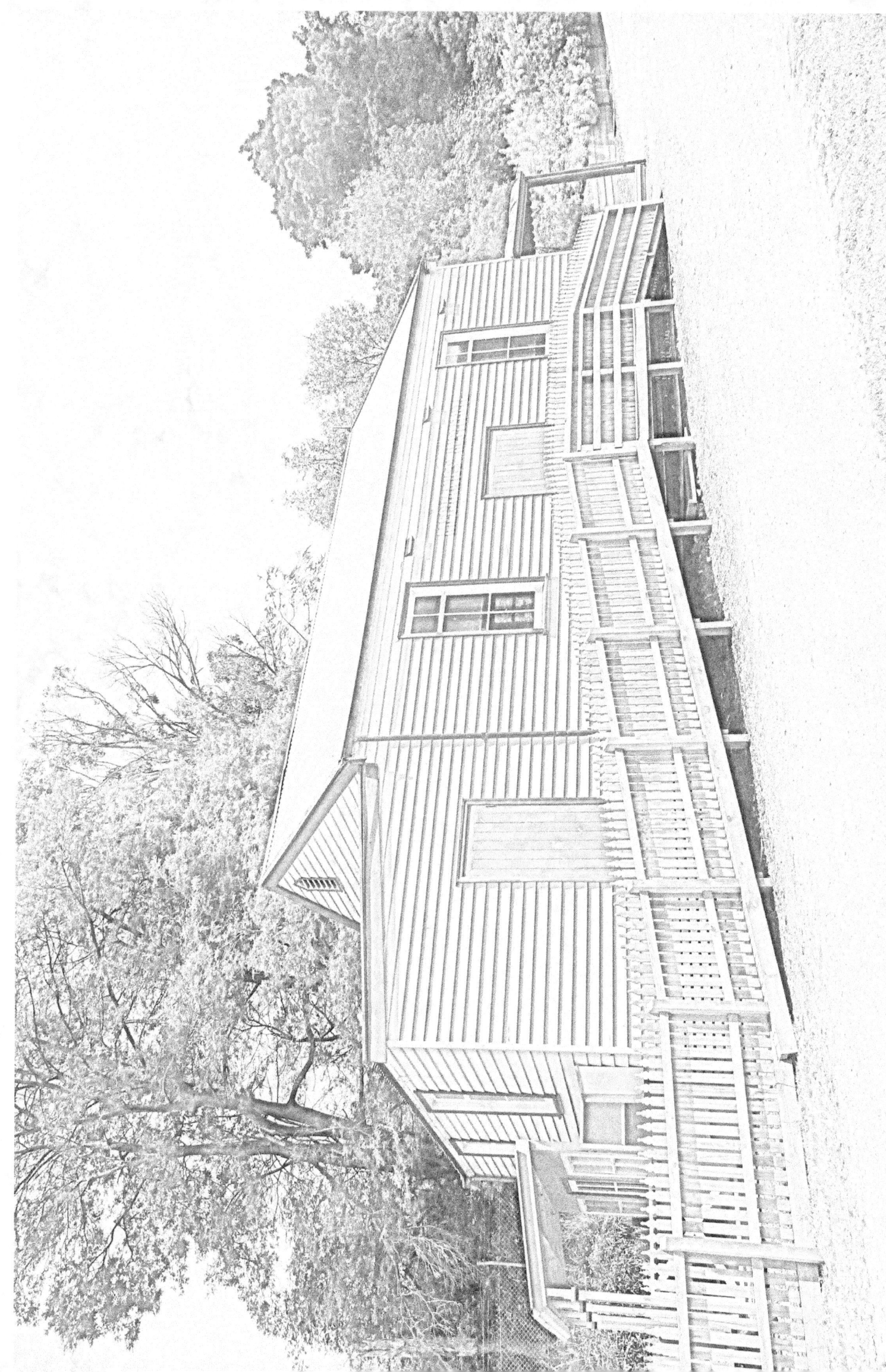

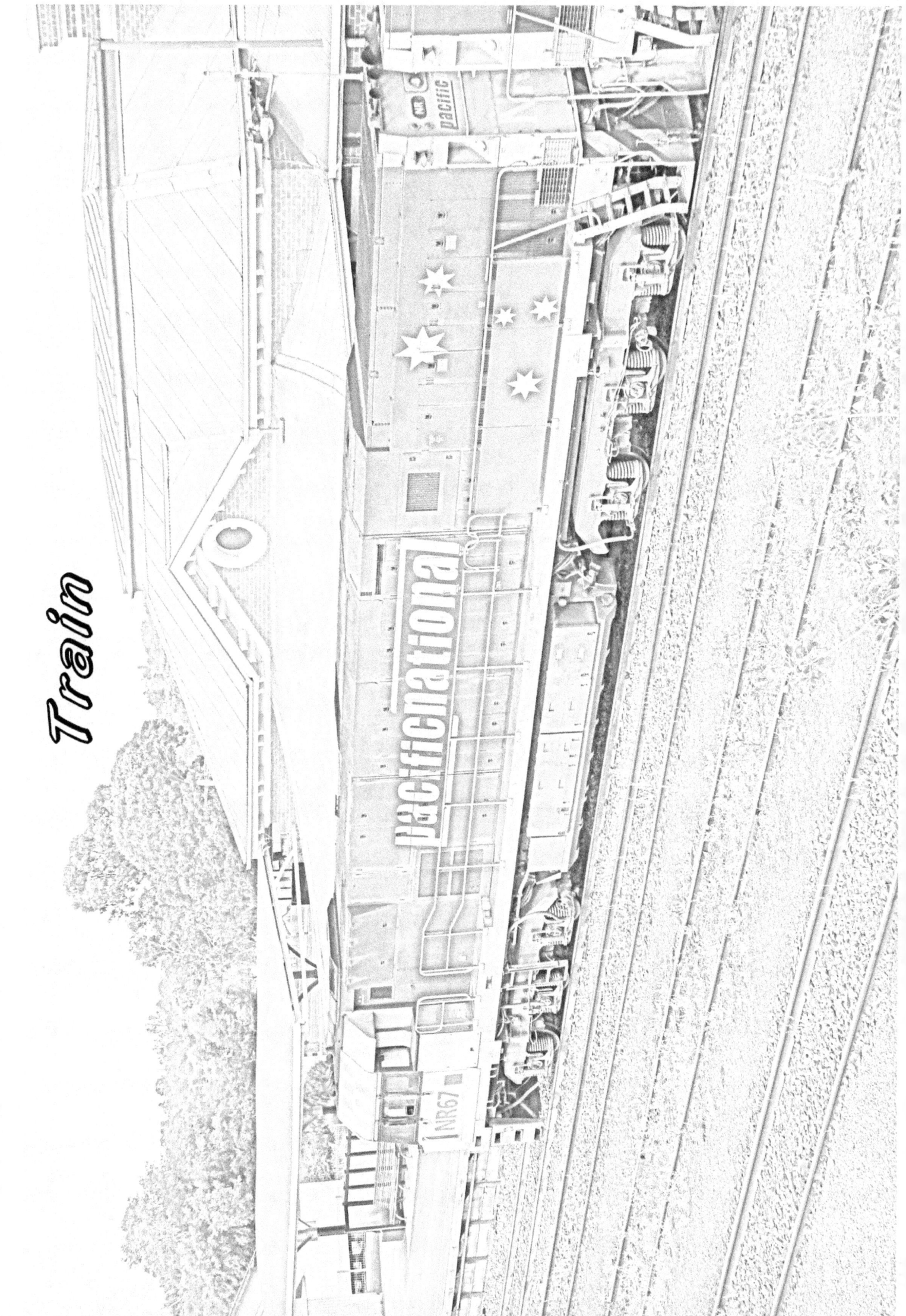

Train

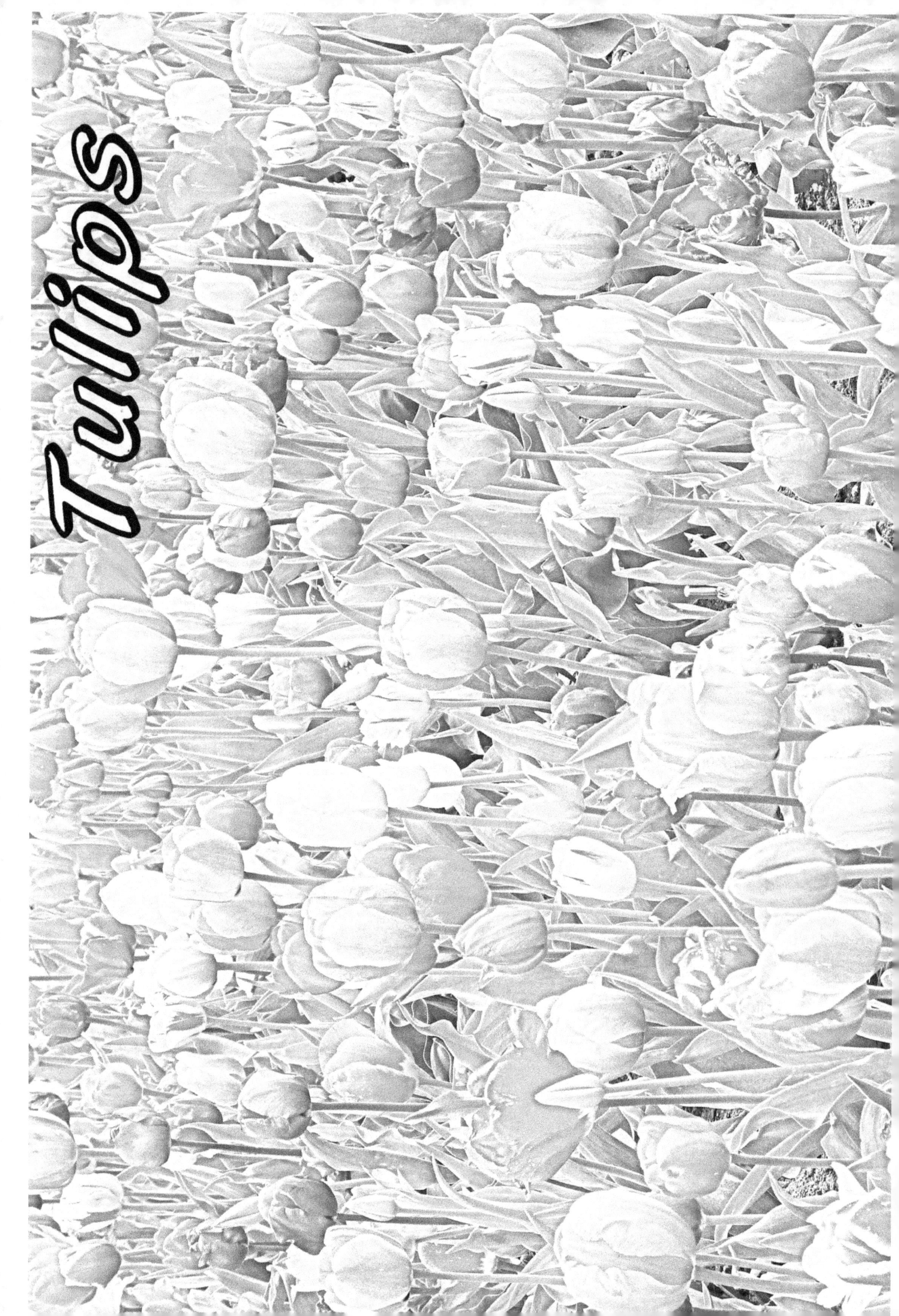

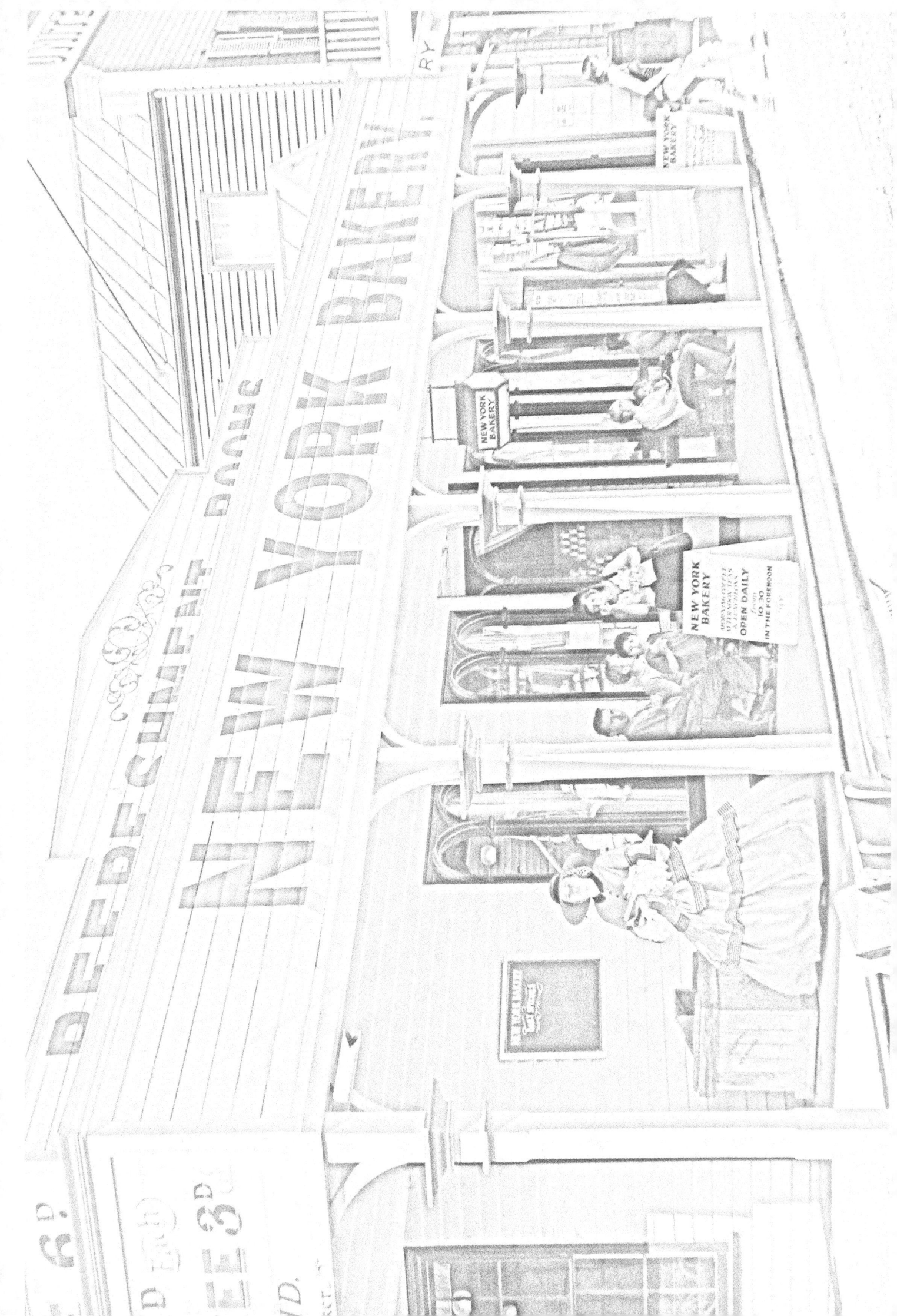

Water Lilly

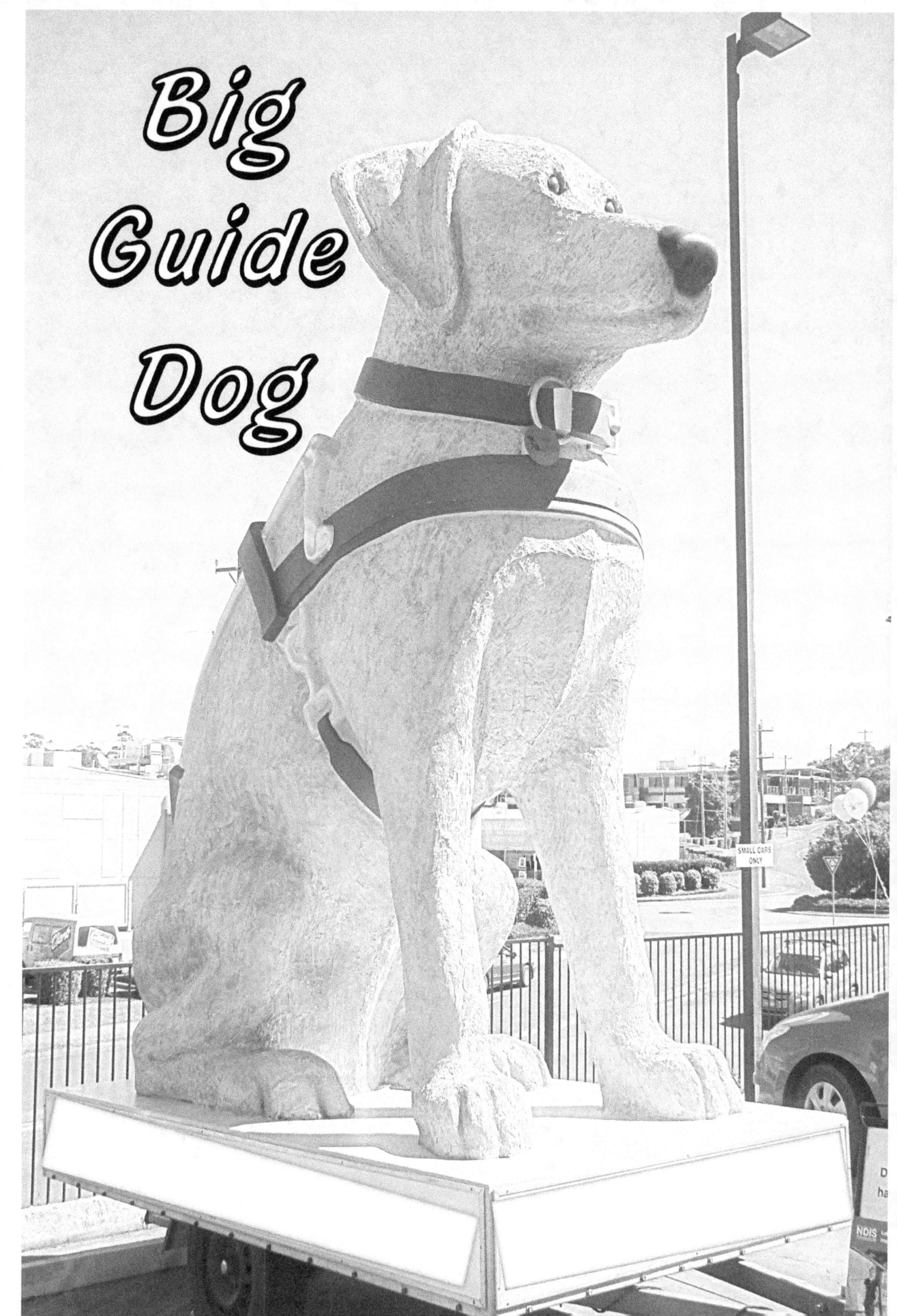

Big Guide Dog

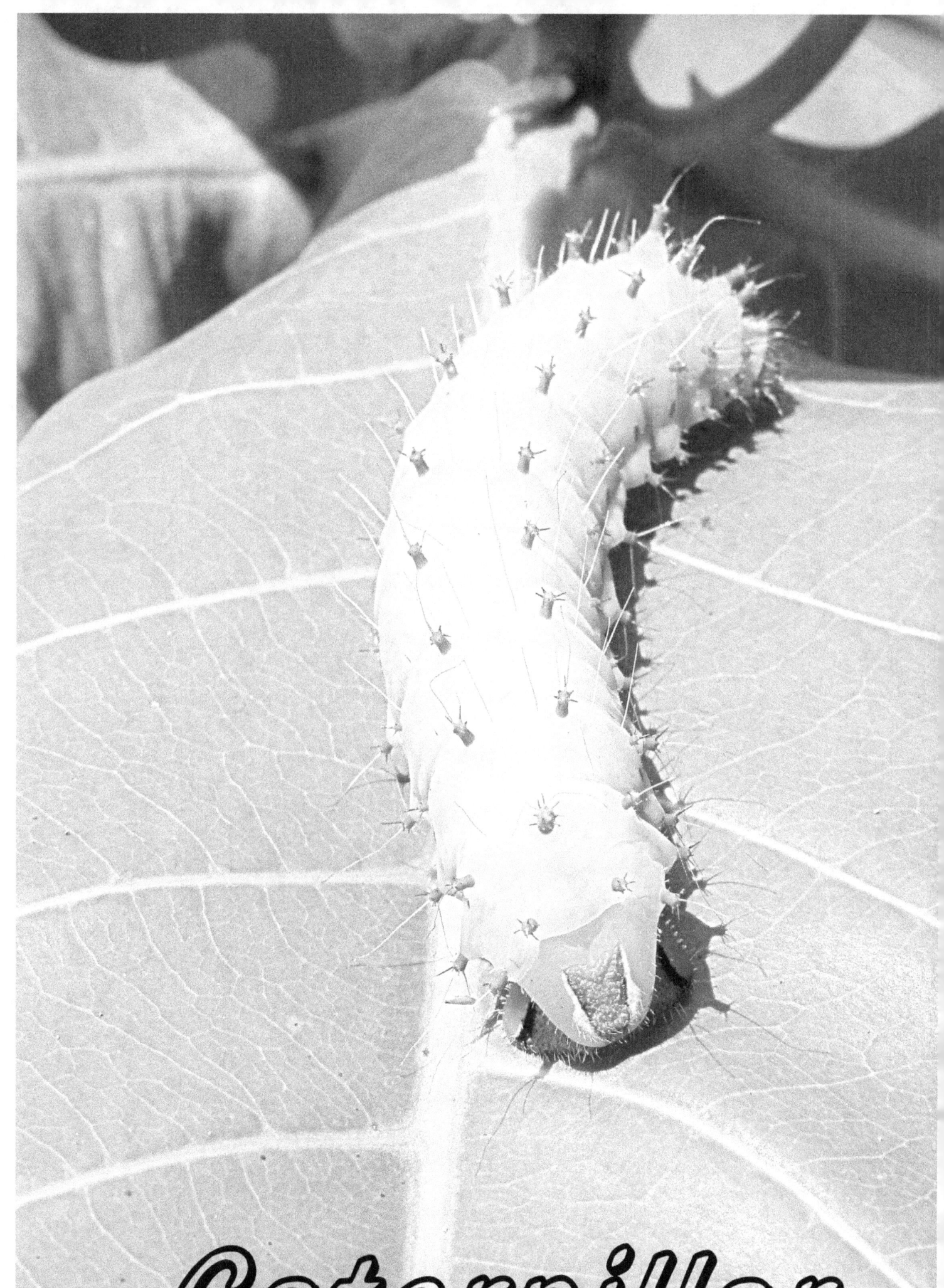

Caterpillar

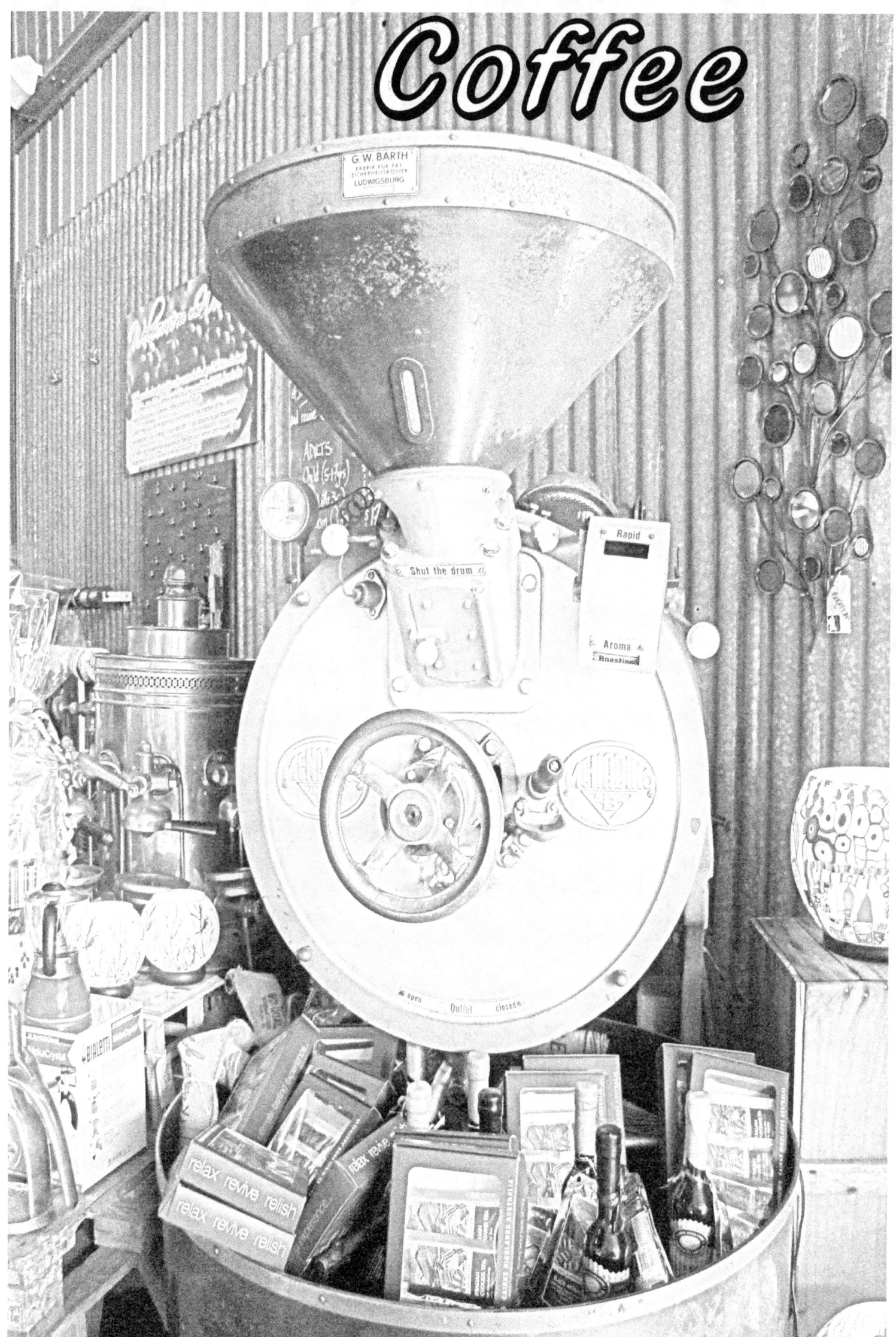

Coffee

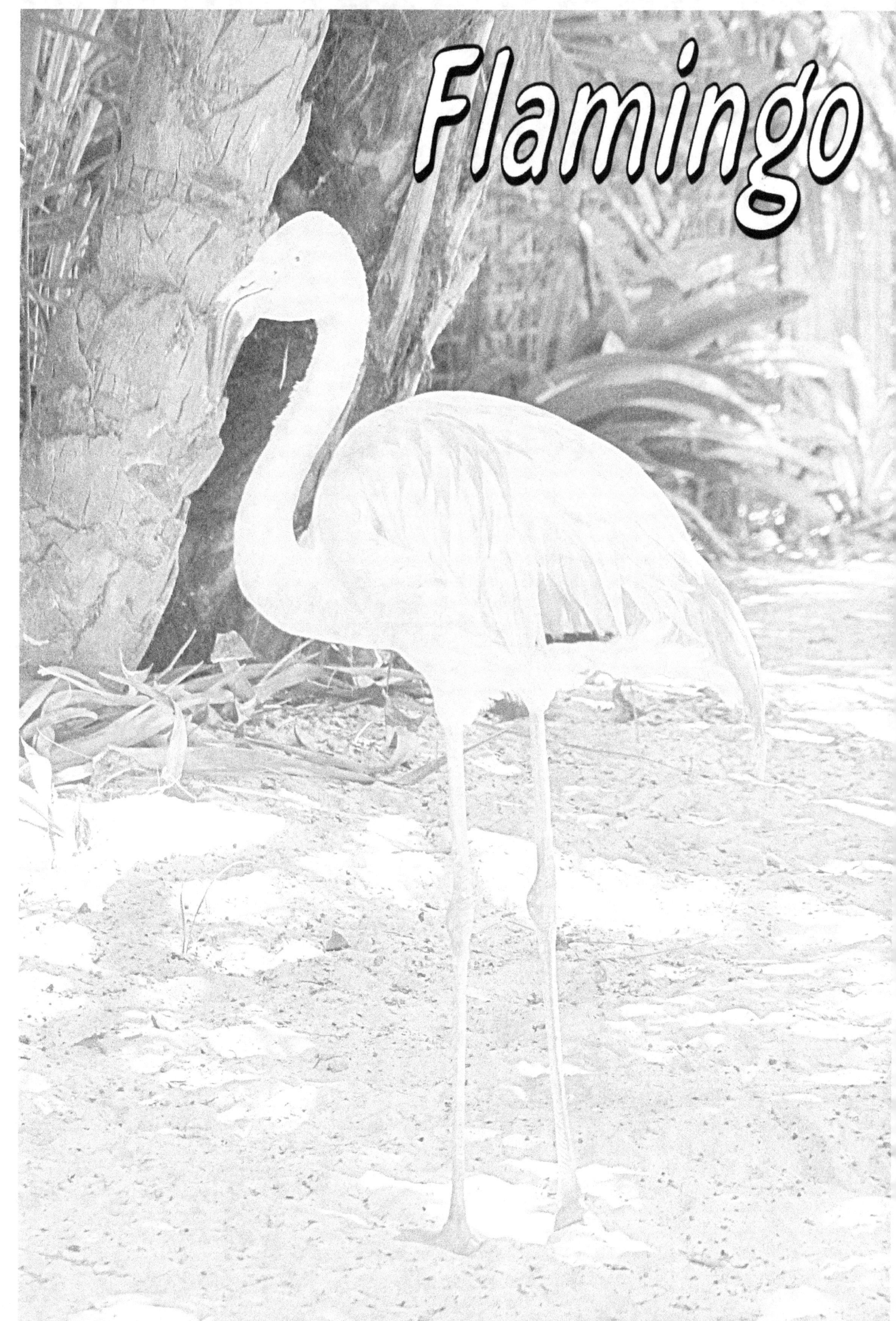

Flamingo

Goose

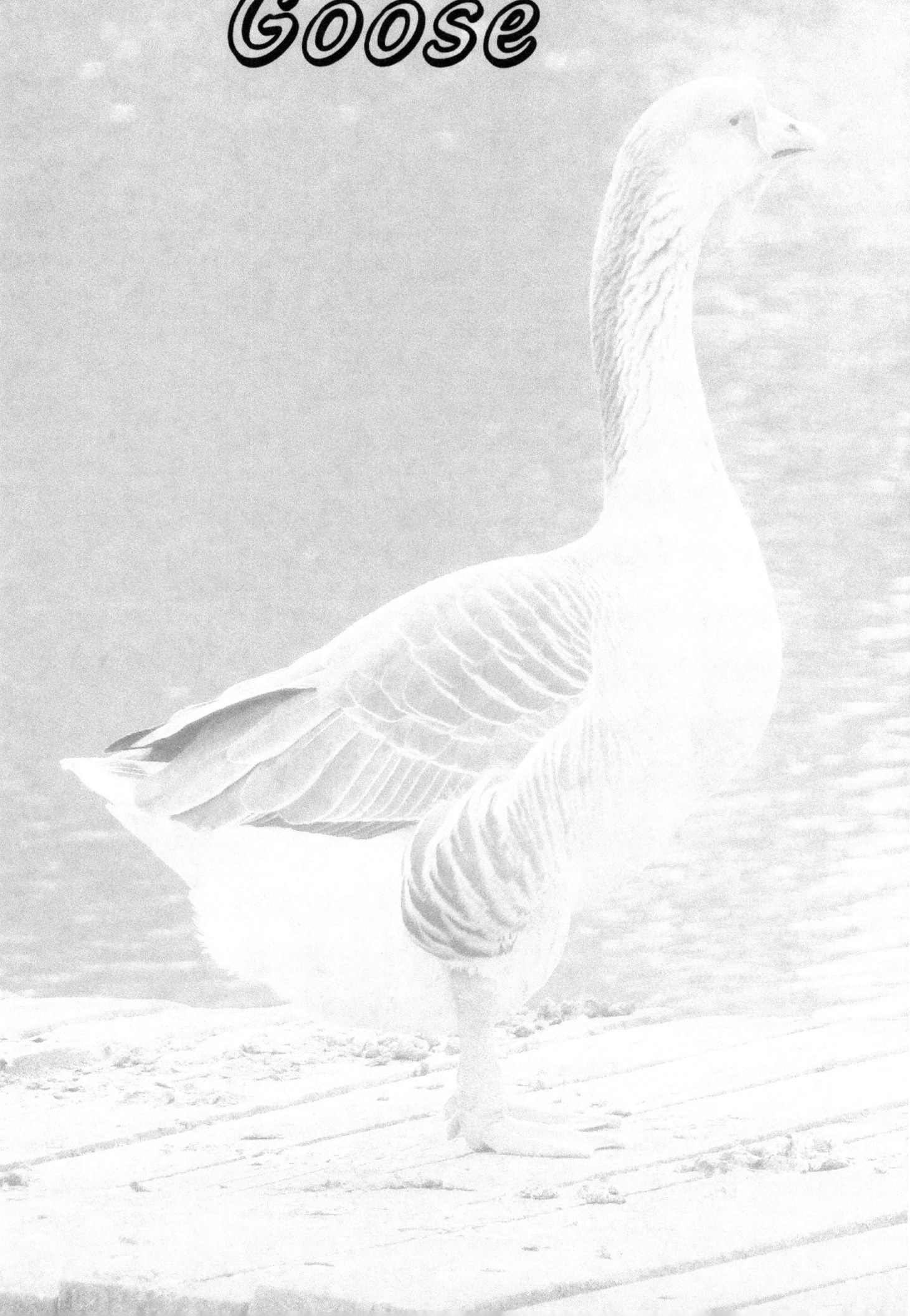

Lighthouse

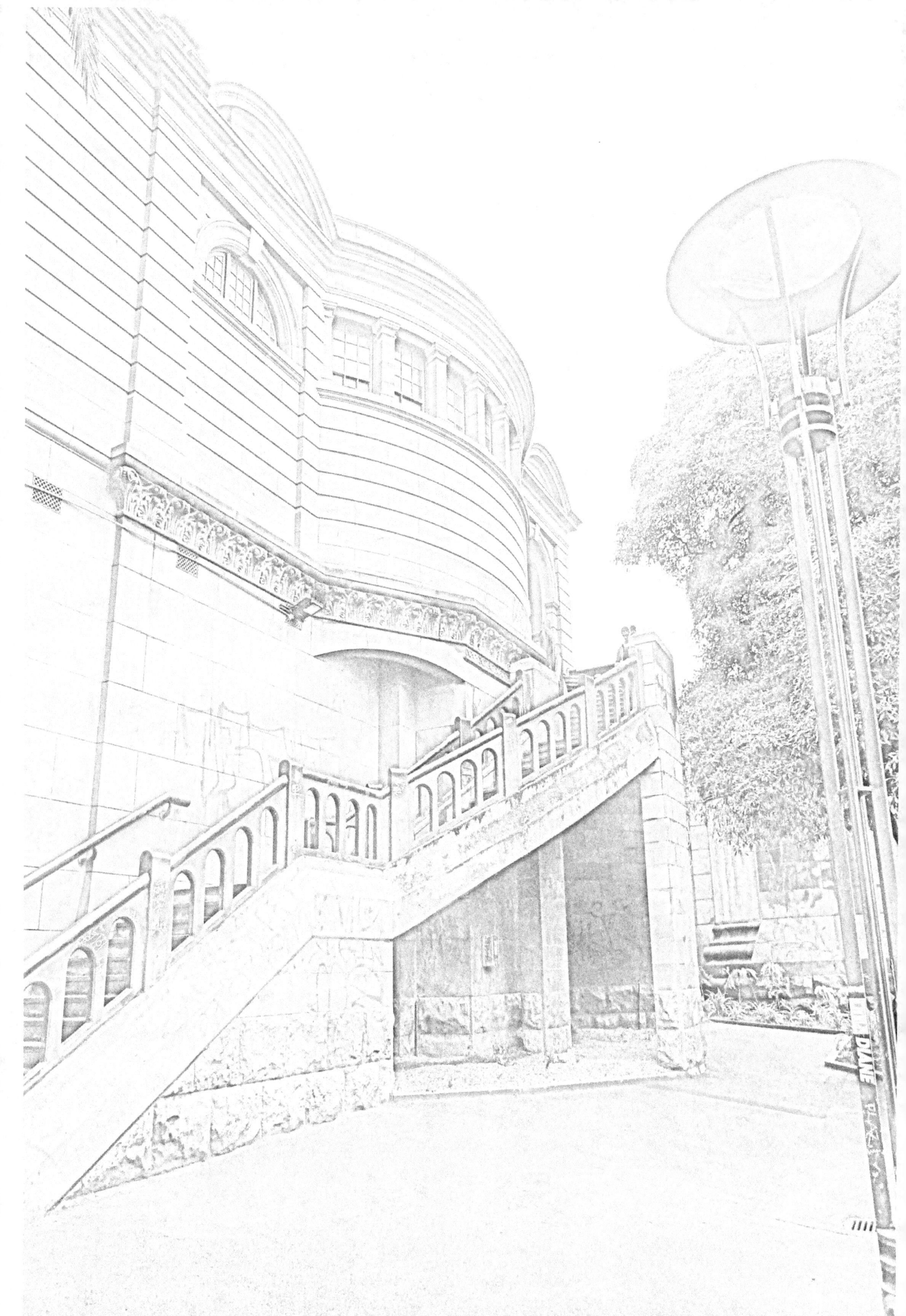

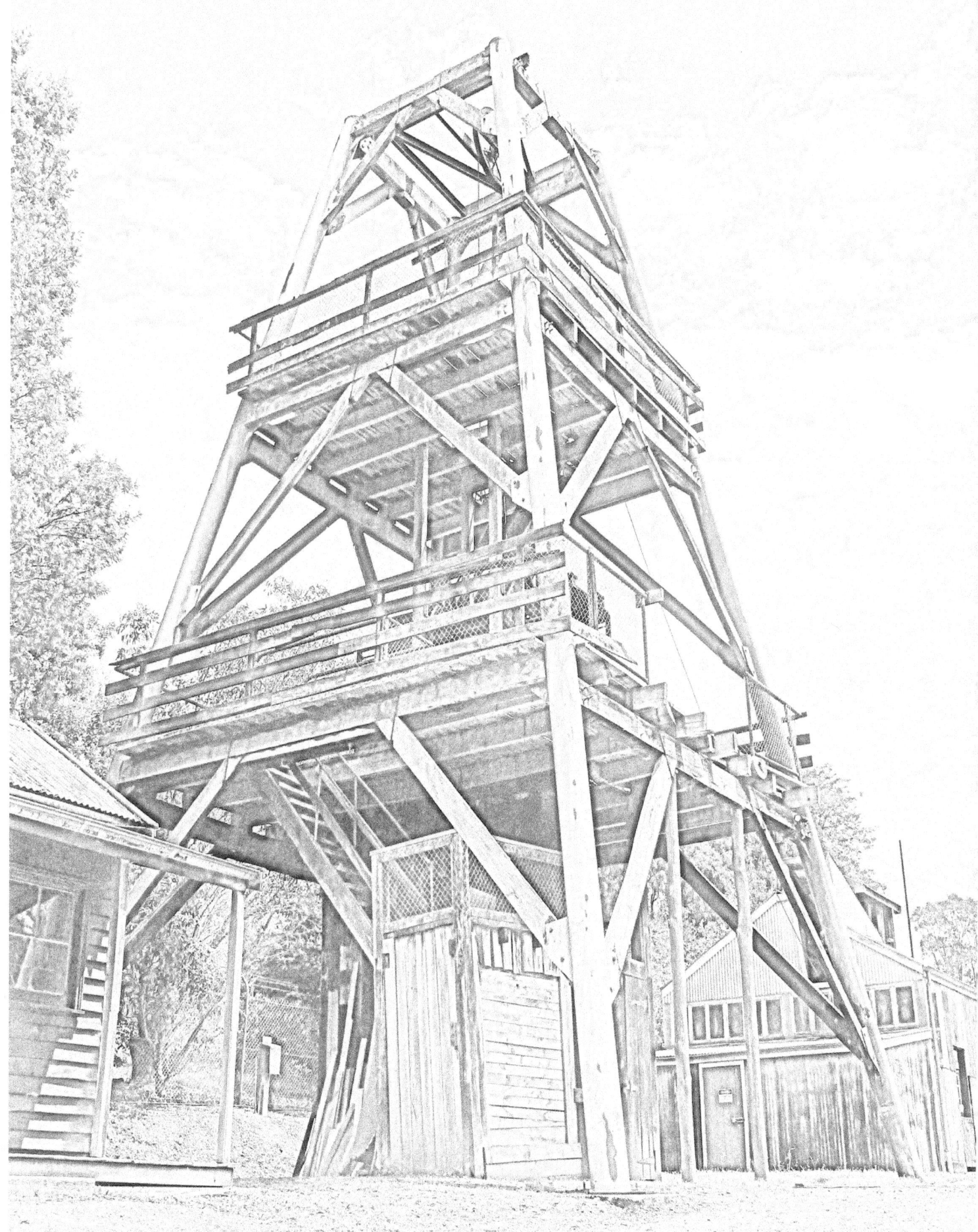

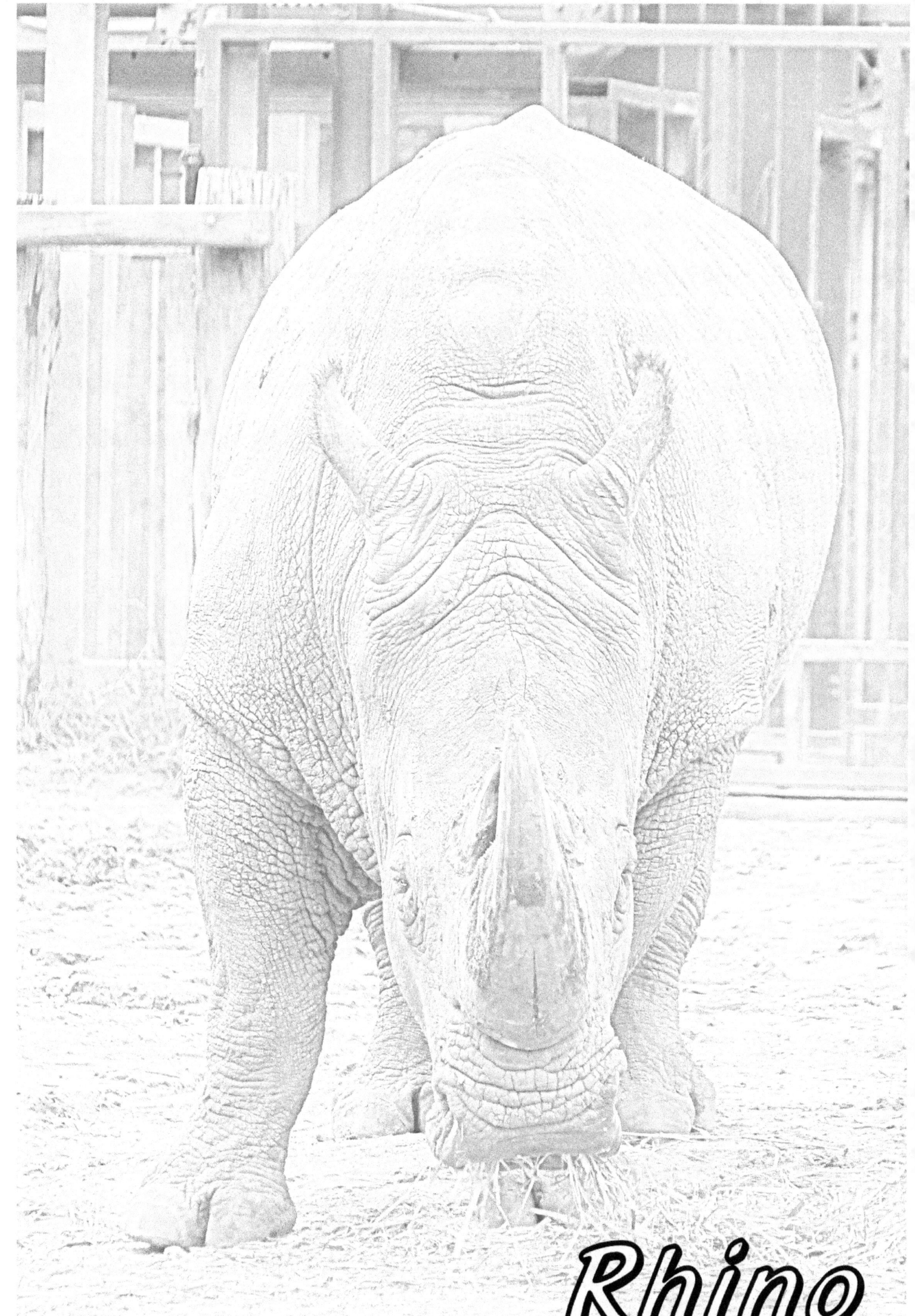

Rhino

www.ingramcontent.com/pod-product-compliance
Lightning Source LLC
Chambersburg PA
CBHW081057180526
45170CB00005B/1797